A WORLD BANK COUNTRY STUDY

# Gender in Bolivian Production

*Reducing Differences in Formality and Productivity of Firms*

**THE WORLD BANK**
Washington, D.C.

Printed on recycled paper

1 2 3 4       12 11 10 09

ISBN-13: 978-0-8213-8014-7
eISBN: 978-0-8213-8016-1
ISSN: 0253-2123       DOI: 10.1596/978-0-8213-8014-7

**Library of Congress Cataloging-in-Publication Data has been requested.**

# Contents

## Tables

## Figures

**Boxes**

# Preface

In Bolivia, women are over-represented in the informal sector, especially in informal self-employment. At the same time, female-owned micro and small firms tend to be more informal and less profitable than male-owned firms. The main objective of this paper is to investigate why businesses owned by women are more informal and less profitable than male-owned firms. A second objective is to identify gender-based productivity constraints that hinder the growth of female-owned businesses. The analysis uses fresh quantitative data from firm surveys, national household surveys, and qualitative data from focus groups.

Bolivian women accelerated their entry into the labor market in recent decades; at the same time, job growth in the formal sector contracted and the informal sector expanded rapidly. Women's low education and protective labor market regulations explain some but not all of the gender differences in formality. Women's disproportionate propensity for self-employment is partly a result of their family responsibilities. Family responsibilities also play a role in women's tendency to concentrate in low-productivity jobs and sectors and result in significant gender wage gaps. Those characteristics of the female labor force—higher informality, less education, and lower wages—are more pronounced for indigenous women.

The main finding of the analysis is that gender-based differences in firms' formality and profitability can be explained by the scale of operation, the sector of operation, education, and the motivation to get into business.

Policy implications of the analysis indicate that since women's businesses are on average too small to reap the full benefits from formalization, they concentrate in low-productivity sectors that earn low profits; their owners have lower average educational attainment than their male counterparts; unlike men, women's motivations for being in business are often shaped by the need to juggle productive and reproductive roles; and they use less financial services, mainly due to more constraints to demand credit.

Policy implications of the analysis indicate that since women's businesses are on average too small to tap the full benefits of formalization, policies should focus on increasing the productivity and scale of female-owned businesses. Two general policy priorities thus emerge: promote women's access to productive assets to facilitate growth and productivity of female-owned businesses, and provide an enabling environment for women's entrepreneurship by expanding women's choices and capacity to respond to market opportunities.

# Acknowledgments

This report was prepared by a core team including Yaye Seynabou Sakho (LCSPE), Trine Lunde (LCSPR), and Maria Arribas-Banos (LCC6) under the guidance and supervision of Rodrigo Chaves (Sector Manager LCSPE) and Carlos Silva-Jauregui (Lead Economist and Sector Leader, PREM). Carlos Felipe Jaramillo (Country Director, LCC6A) linked the team to the Bank's overall strategy. Mauricio Carrizosa (Adviser, IEG) provided guidance and comments on the earlier draft of the report.

The report was based on contributions from David McKenzie (DECRG), Lykke Andersen (INESAD Bolivia), Beatriz Muriel (INESAD, Bolivia), and Ruth Llanos (LCCBO). The peer reviewers for this report are Nadereh Chamlou (Senior Advisor, MENA), Elena Bardasi (Senior Economist, PREMGE), and Omar Arias (Sector Leader, HD LC6).

The report benefited from excellent production support from Michael Geller (LCSPE). Chris Humphrey (Consultant) provided editorial input. Patricia Chacon Holt (LCSPE) and Monica Torrelio (LCCBO) supported the production process of the report at different stages.

Financial support provided by the Gender Action Plan (GAP) for the preparation of the report is gratefully acknowledged.

This report was enhanced by substantive comments from a variety of people during various stages of this project. Comments were received from: Julio Loayza (LCCBO), Julio Velasco (LCCBO), Maria Beatriz Orlando (Senior Economist, LCSPR), Wendy Cunningham (LSCHS), Elizabeth Katz (Associate Professor, University of Los Angeles), David McKenzie (DECRG), Marco Scuriatti (LC6), and Vicente Fretes Cibils (former Lead Economist and PREM Sector Leader LCSPE).

Carmen Carpio and Jorge Gamarra (Knowledge Management Team), Natalia Torres (Universidad de los Andes, Colombia), and the Knowledge Management team are gratefully acknowledged for the excellent efforts to produce the video supporting the dissemination of the study.

Encuestas y Estudios is acknowledged for collecting the qualitative and quantitative data.

The report was prepared based on two missions in Bolivia that took place in October 2006 and February 2007. The team would like to thank the Bolivian authorities, including UDAPE, INE, the Vice Ministry of Women Affairs, Ministry of Planning through VIPFE, and the Vice Ministry of Planning and Coordination for their cooperation in delineating the scope of the study and facilitating access to all the information necessary for the study. The team gratefully acknowledges all the support received.

# Executive Summary

In this paper,[1] we seek to better understand gender-based differences in firms' tendencies toward formality, the impact of formality on profits, and the productivity of small informal firms. To this end, we conduct a gender analysis of firms' formality and productivity in six different sectors in Bolivia. The findings shed new light on gender-based differences in the determinants of a firm's decision to become formal and the consequences of this decision for profits. The findings also shed light on the constraints to productivity in small and micro enterprises and how these may vary depending on the gender of the business owner.

Women are over-represented in the informal sector, especially in informal self-employment. Almost two-thirds (65 percent) of the urban female labor force was employed informally—defined as being employed in, or running, businesses without a tax registration number—in 2005, compared with only 57 percent of the male labor force. Women in the informal sector also have a higher tendency toward self-employment than men. In 2005, 77 percent of women in the informal sector were self-employed, versus 58 percent of men. Bolivian women have one of the highest rates of both labor market participation and informality in Latin America.

Female-owned micro and small firms also tend to be more informal and less profitable than male-owned firms. Our empirical analysis indicates that only 46 percent of female-owned firms have a municipal license compared with 60 percent of male-owned firms; in addition, only 22 percent of female-owned firms have a tax number compared with 33 percent of male-owned firms. Female owners also earn lower profits on average: their mean monthly profits are 1,202 Bs, as against 2,127 Bs for male owners.

A main goal of this study is to determine the variables responsible for the lower formality of women-owned businesses. The companion study (World Bank 2007a) shows that Bolivia's informal sector is the largest in Latin America by many definitions and measures. It also provides a rationale for promoting formality given the many negative effects of a high rate of informality. These negative effects include a lower growth potential as informal firms tend to be less productive owing to limited access to physical, financial, and human capital, and a smaller scale of operations; negative fiscal impacts as informal firms "free ride" on services provided with fiscal resources; and negative social externalities, including weaker rule of law and public institutions, increased corruption, and weakened ability to enforce contracts.

A second goal of this study is to identify gender-based productivity constraints that hinder the growth of female-owned businesses. First, our analysis of the impact of formality on profitability shows that the gains of formalization for most female-owned businesses increase as the firms grow. Second, we find that the smaller scale of operation of female-owned firms is one of the main causes of gender-based differences in productivity and profitability. However, most of the differences between male and female-owned firms diminish or disappear as firms grow.

To better understand gender-based differences and constraints, we combine quantitative data from firm and household surveys with qualitative data from focus groups. The quantitative analysis is based on new data from a quantitative survey of 629 formal and informal firms in six industries, as well as data from the 2005 *Encuesta de Mejoramiento de Condiciones de Vida* (MECOVI) household survey. The qualitative analysis is based on 20 focus group discussions held with female and male small- and micro-firm owners in La Paz, El Alto, Cochabamba, and Santa Cruz. The survey provides empirical evidence on the determinants of formality at the firm level and the effects of formality on firm profitability. The qualitative analysis validates findings on the main constraints to formalization and higher productivity.

Throughout the report, tax registration is used as a measure of formality unless otherwise stated. More specifically, workers employed in businesses without a tax registration number (NIT) and self-employed workers who operate businesses without an NIT are informal. The formal workforce consists of workers employed in businesses with an NIT or in a public sector institution; and self-employed workers who operate their businesses with an NIT. This definition differs from the legalistic approach based on social security coverage as well as the productive definition based on worker characteristics and firm size. Survey results indicate that formality follows a continuum, starting with businesses obtaining municipal licenses, and then getting a tax number, and finally signing up with the national firm registry. Of the 630 firms surveyed—which are census representative at the urban level—less than half were completely informal, 28 percent had only a municipal license, 21 percent had a tax number and a municipal license, and only 4 percent had a license, tax number, and were in the national firm registry.

### Women are disproportionately represented in the informal sector as self-employed

Bolivian women accelerated their entry into the labor market in recent decades; at the same time, job growth in formal sectors contracted and the informal sector expanded rapidly. The increase in female labor force participation was driven largely by falling fertility rates and the rapid urbanization initiated in Bolivia in the 1950s. By 2005, nearly 44 percent of the Bolivian workforce was female, up from 33 percent in 1980. The country's rapid urbanization also fostered the growth of a large informal sector, and by the mid-1970s, 57 percent of total urban employment was informal. In the 1980s, a shrinking public sector further boosted informal employment to about 60 percent of the urban labor force, the level at which it remained in 2005. With a shrinking public sector and a decreasing tendency to hire women in the formal private sector, the share of women in the informal sector increased.

Women's low education and protective labor market regulations explain some but not all of the gender differences in formality. Rigid labor regulation and women's lower educational attainment are the main constraints to women obtaining formal jobs, especially in the private sector. Women are mandated to work a shorter workweek, are not permitted to work at night, and employer-paid maternity benefits cannot be shared by husbands. At the same time, provisions against discrimination in remuneration and merit promotion are weakly enforced. Women in formal employment have similar levels of education as men, but in the informal sector women have on average 1.7 years less schooling than men, and two years less for self-employed women. However, these factors do not fully explain the high informality of women.

Domestic responsibilities and marital status seem to shape women's labor market outcomes by creating a need for the flexibility commonly associated with informal self-employment. Employment outcomes for women are, for instance, more sensitive to marital status than for men. While married and divorced women are much more likely to be informally employed than men, single women's labor market outcomes mirror those of their male peers. This suggests that family and domestic responsibilities may influence married women's preference for the added flexibility of informal self-employment.

The sizable gender wage gaps found in Bolivia are also explained by the tendency of women to concentrate in low-productivity jobs and sectors, together with their lower educational attainment. Overall gender-based wage gaps are due in part to the concentration of women in low-productivity sectors—the result of preferences, social expectations, or gender stereotypes—while gender gaps within sectors are due to women's lower educational achievement and concentration in lower-skill jobs.

The characteristics of the female labor force—such as higher informality, less education, and lower wages—are more pronounced for indigenous women. More than 60 percent of indigenous women engage in informal self-employment, compared with less than 40 percent of indigenous men, 40 percent of non-indigenous women, and only 28 percent of non-indigenous men. Informally self-employed indigenous women earn about 67 percent of an indigenous man's average hourly wage, and only 60 percent of what non-indigenous women earn. Indigenous women's higher rates of informality and lower earnings largely reflect the effects of ethnic and gender-based education gaps.

*Gender-based differences in formality and profitability can be explained by the scale of operation, the sector of operation, education, and the motivation to get into business*

Female-owned firms operate on a smaller scale. Male-owned businesses have on average three times the assets of female-owned businesses, and employ 3.5 people compared with 2.7 for female-owned businesses. A smaller scale of operation affords women more flexibility to care for their families and to adapt the business to shifting demand and to the income cycle of their husbands. Operating out of the home also allows them to balance home and working responsibilities, which limits their ability to expand. Women small- and micro-firm owners are twice as likely to operate out of the home as men.

Female-owned small and micro businesses are on average too small to reap many benefits from formalization. While formality is associated with greater profitability in small firms (three and five workers), the impact of formality on profitability is negative for micro firms (less than three workers). For this group, the negative impact on profitability is perhaps the greatest "constraint" to seeking formality. Attempts at increasing the formality of both micro and large firms should thus focus on reducing the costs of formality and increasing its benefits. Given the high share of female-owned business that are too small to reap any benefits from formality, stimulating the growth of female-owned businesses would also boost their incentives for formalizing. Many gender-based differences in how firms operate diminish or disappear as firms grow.

Once female-owned businesses grow beyond a certain size, gender-based differences in the use of financial services, in access to physical capital, and in propensity to hire female employees, seem to disappear. The cut-off size where gender differences disappear is 11 or more employees.

Women concentrate their businesses in low-productivity sectors. Ninety five percent of female-owned businesses surveyed operate in four out of the six sectors surveyed: groceries stores, food vending, alpaca wool production, and textiles and clothing manufacturing. Conversely, 64 percent of male-owned businesses surveyed operate in the wood manufacturing and transport sectors, where female-owned firms account for only 2-3 percent of the total. The four sectors in which women concentrate are also the ones where profits are low and gender-based differences in profits are substantial.

Female firm owners in the informal sector have lower average educational attainment than their male counterparts, with some variation across sectors. Male firm owners have on average 2.2 more years of schooling than women. This is not only a direct constraint on productivity but also an indirect constraint as it may affect women's ability to apply for and use financial services. In addition, our empirical analysis indicates that women tend to hire other women, so that low educational levels become a constraint throughout female-owned firms.

Unlike men, women's motivations for being in business are often shaped by their need to juggle productive and reproductive roles. Self-employed female business owners rank "the ability to care for children and elders while working" significantly higher then male business owners among the reasons for being self employed. When assessing constraints on firm productivity, women also rank domestic responsibilities higher than men. In the words of one female firm owner: *"A woman has to work triple: the home, the children and in addition, the business. This particular line of work allows me to take care of my home and my children and I don't have to leave my house."* Furthermore, qualitative data show that married women tend to view their business activity as a complement to their husband's income, not as a business venture in its own right.

Women's desire to expand their businesses is strong in some sectors but is lower than men's on average. For instance, women in textiles expressed a strong wish to expand—a logical aspiration given that doubling the capital of women in this sector would increase monthly profits by about 22 percent. However, this desire may be hampered by a lack of access to financial and physical capital.

The quantitative data show that gender differences in the use of financial services also narrows as firms grow, while qualitative data suggest that demand-side constraints play a major role in limiting women's access to finance. Women tend to use less formal credit and other financial services. Yet, qualitative data suggest that women do not perceive any gender-based discrimination against women in the supply of credit from financial institutions. Rather, constraints to women's access to credit and use of financial services seem to be demand-side driven, including difficulties in documenting income and collateral and lack of information on how to deal with loan procedures.

The qualitative data suggest that restrictions on women's autonomy may dampen the productivity of female-owned businesses. The qualitative evidence shows that women's mobility is constrained by traditional gender roles, typically in the form of a husband's wish that the woman stay at home.

*Policy implications of the analysis indicate that the focus should be on alleviating gender-based productivity constraints.*

The implications for policy of increasing formality and profitability of female-owned micro enterprises focus on alleviating gender-based productivity constraints. Since women's businesses are on average too small to tap the full benefits of formalization, policies should focus on increasing the productivity and scale of female-owned businesses. Two general policy priorities thus emerge: promote women's access to productive assets to facilitate growth and productivity of female-owned businesses, and provide an enabling environment for women's entrepreneurship by expanding women's choices and capacity to respond to market opportunities. Initiatives to increase access to productive assets include facilitating women's access to credit, formal property rights, training and education; Initiatives to provide an enabling environment include promotion of associative activities, provision of child care and further assessments of the root causes of women's segregation into certain low-productivity sectors and occupations.

Specific interventions targeted to female-owned small and micro enterprises include the following:

- Short term:
  - Facilitate female firm owners' use of formal credit and other financial services by alleviating demand-side constraints through information and marketing campaigns (e.g., how to fill out loan applications and how to gather supporting documentation). The authorities may also want to assess gender differences in the distribution of formal land and property rights—commonly used as collateral—and how this affects women's use of credit.
  - Promote business associations and other organizations that help female business owners build entrepreneurial ability and self-sufficiency and create scope for women to share experiences, discuss common concerns, and lobby together to seek solutions.

- Medium term:
  - Improve access to managerial training and business linkage programs and strengthen assistance in accessing new markets (e.g., niche markets, export markets, public procurement) with competitive products. In all policy areas, the authorities should take into account sector-specific considerations and solutions and give special attention to the needs of indigenous women.
  - Promote access to childcare for working mothers who would like to expand the scale of their businesses but who are constrained by inadequate or non-existent childcare services. The government should conduct an assessment of interest in such a program and study how to design a pilot and estimate the fiscal cost of the intervention.

- Medium to long term:
  - Close gender gaps in formal education that limit both women's entrepreneurial capability and their ability to enter formal employment. Focus especially on addressing multiple inequalities suffered by indigenous women.
  - Address root causes for gender-based occupational segregation and gender stereotypes to make the choice of entering informal and/or low-productivity sectors and occupations a matter of true preference.

## Notes

[1] A companion study to the World Bank report "Policies for Increasing Firms' Formality and Productivity" (2007a).

# Abbreviations and Acronyms

| | |
|---|---|
| AFP | *Administradora de Fondo de Pensiones* (Pension Funds Administrators) |
| ASOFIN | *Asociación de Entidades Financieras Especializadas en Micro Finanzas de Bolivia* (Association of Bolivian Financial Entities Specializing in Micro-Finance) |
| BCB | *Banco Central de Bolivia* (Central Bank of Bolivia) |
| CEPROBOL | *Centro de Promoción Bolivia* (Confederation of Private Businessmen) |
| CG | Consultative Group |
| DFID | Department for International Development (UK) |
| FONDESIF | *Fondo de Desarrollo del Sistema Financiero y de Apoyo al Sector Productivo* (Fund for the Development of the Financial Sector and for Support to the Productive Sector) |
| GDP | Gross Domestic Product |
| IDA | International Development Association |
| IDB | Inter-American Development Bank |
| ILO | International Labour Organization |
| IMF | International Monetary Fund |
| INE | *Instituto Nacional de Estadística* (National Statistics Institute) |
| MAS | *Movimiento al Socialismo* (Movement to Socialism) |
| MDGs | Millennium Development Goals |
| MDRI | Multilateral Debt Relief Initiative |
| MECOVI | *Encuesta de Mejoramiento de Condiciones de Vida* (Survey on Improvement in Living Conditions) |
| MEFs | Microfinance Entities |
| NAFIBO | *Nacional Financiera Boliviana* (Bolivian National Financial Fund) |
| NGO | Nongovernmental Organization |
| NIT | Tax Enrollment Number |
| OECD | Organization for Economic Cooperation and Development |
| PFFs | Private Financial Funds |
| PRSP | Poverty Reduction Strategy Paper |
| SBEF | *Superintendencia de Bancos y Entidades Financieras* (Superintendency of Banks and Financial Entities of Bolivia) |
| SIG | *Sistema de Información Geográphica* (Geographic Information System) |
| SIN | *Servicio de Impuestos Nacionales* (National Tax Service) |
| UDAPE | *Unidad de Análisis de Políticas Económicas y Sociales* (Economic and Social Policies Analysis Unit) |
| UNDP | United Nations Development Programme |
| USAID | United States Agency for International Development |

**Republic of Bolivia Fiscal Year**
January 1 to December 31

**Currency Equivalents**
(as of September 28, 2007)
Currency Unit = Bolivianos
1 U.S. Dollar = Bs 8.00

**Weights and Measures**
Metric System

| | |
|---|---|
| Vice President, LCR: | Pamela Cox |
| Director, LCC6C: | Carlos Felipe Jaramillo |
| Director, LCSPR: | Marcelo Giugale |
| Sector Manager, LCSPE: | Rodrigo Chaves |
| Sector Leader, LCSPE: | Carlos Silva-Jauregui |
| Task Team Leaders: | Seynabou Sakho, Maria Arribas-Banos |

# CHAPTER 1

# Men and Women in Bolivia's Informal Sector

The informal sector in Bolivia is among the largest in Latin America, with women over-represented, especially in informal self-employment. In this chapter, we look at differences between men and women in terms of their employment in formal and informal firms. Our analysis is based mainly on the nationally representative 2005 MECOVI household survey. It defines informality as being employed in firms without a tax registration number (NIT) or in self-employment without registration with the tax authorities.

## Trends in Informality and Female Employment

Informality in Bolivia is high and has been so for the last 30 years. Using the legal definition based on pension system coverage, 70 percent of the urban employed labor force in Bolivia is engaged in the informal sector (World Bank 2007a). Together with Paraguay, this is the highest in the region. The rapid urbanization process initiated in the 1950s fostered the development of the informal sector and by the mid 1970s, 57 percent of urban employment was already informal. In the 1980s, substantial restructuring—including privatization of state enterprises and reductions in the state workforce—further boosted informal employment to about 60 percent of the urban labor force, the level that still prevailed in 2005.

While the participation of women in the labor force grew rapidly in recent decades, it was not accompanied by job growth and expansion of opportunities for women in the formal sectors. With falling dependency burdens attributable to a lower fertility rate, women's entry into the labor force accelerated, so that by 2005, women constituted 43.5 percent of the Bolivian workforce, up from 33 percent in 1980.[1] But the rapid rise in female employment was concentrated in the informal sector, while the formal private sector continued to largely exclude women. In 2005, women accounted for nearly half of all informal sector jobs in 2005, yet only 38 percent of formal sector jobs (Figure 1.1).

**Figure 1.1. Female Share of Labor Force, by Employment Category (2005)**

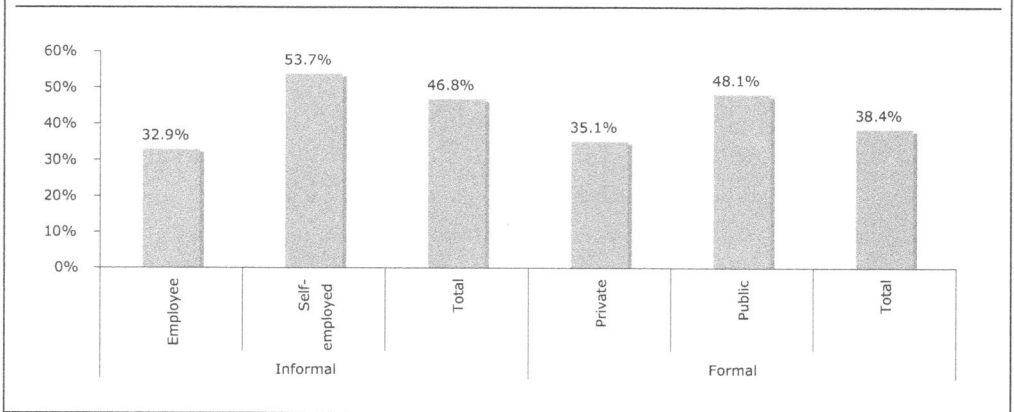

*Source:* Authors' calculation based on the 2005 MECOVI.

Women are overrepresented in the informal sector where the vast majority is self-employed. Nearly two-thirds (65 percent) of the urban female labor force was employed informally in 2005, either as salaried workers or self-employed, compared with 57 percent of the male labor force (Figure 1.2). In 2005, 77 percent of women in the informal sector were self-employed, compared with 58 percent of men.

**Figure 1.2. Male and Female Urban Labor Forces, by Employment Category (%)**

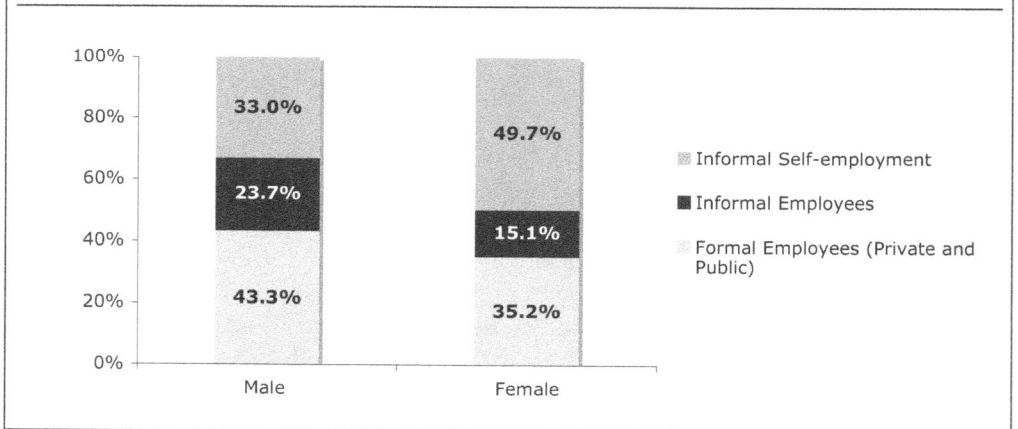

*Source:* Authors' calculation based on MECOVI (2005).

Relative to women in other countries in Latin America, Bolivian women are economically more active. Bolivian women have one of the highest rates of labor market participation and of informality in Latin America (Figure 1.3). The numbers are based on definition of the informal or 'low-productivity' sector used by the Economic Commission for Latin America and the Caribbean (ECLAC), which includes the self-employed and those employed in domestic services and micro enterprises with less than five employees.

**Figure 1.3. Female Labor Force Participation and Informality in LAC (2000–02, for Urban Areas)**

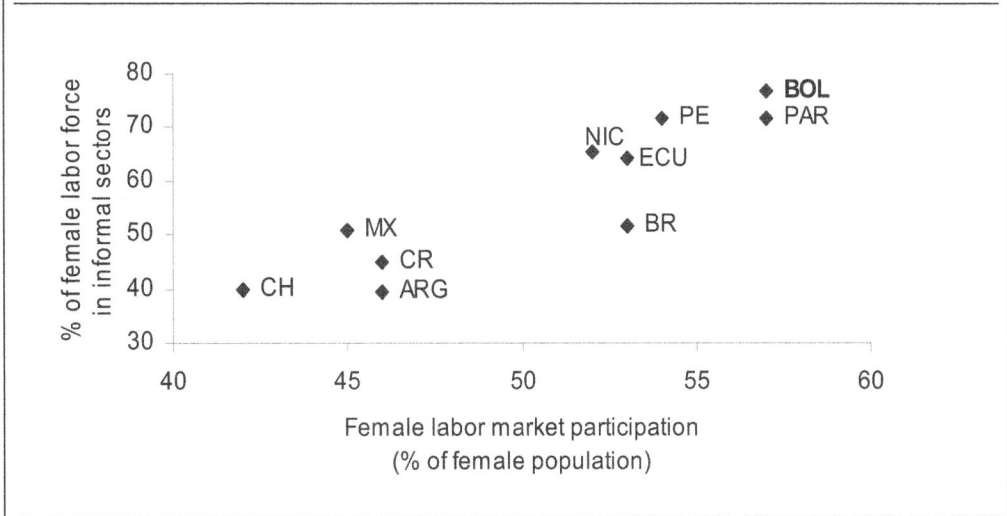

*Source:* ECLAC 2007a.

## Factors Shaping Gender Labor Force Trends: Domestic Pressures, Education, Regulation

Higher rates of informal work and self-employment among women appear to be driven largely by women's need to balance home and work responsibilities The persistent family responsibilities of women are often irreconcilable with formal work schedules, and the flexibility offered by self-employment helps balance productive and reproductive roles (World Bank 2005, Cunningham and Gomez 2004, Tannuri-Pianto and Pianto 2003). Employment outcomes for women are more sensitive to marital status and household composition (the presence of young children). The participation rates of single women are similar to those of men in both formal employment and self-employment, confirming a regional trend that shows higher participation rates in the formal sector for unmarried women without children—in most cases equal to or higher than that of men (Cunningham 2001). Married women, on the other hand, are much more likely to be self-employed than married men (Figure 1.4). Tannuri-Pianto and others (2004) find that having young children (less than six years old) increases the probability of Bolivian women being self-employed.

**Figure 1.4. Share of Informal Self-Employment in All Employment, by Gender and Marital Status, 2005**

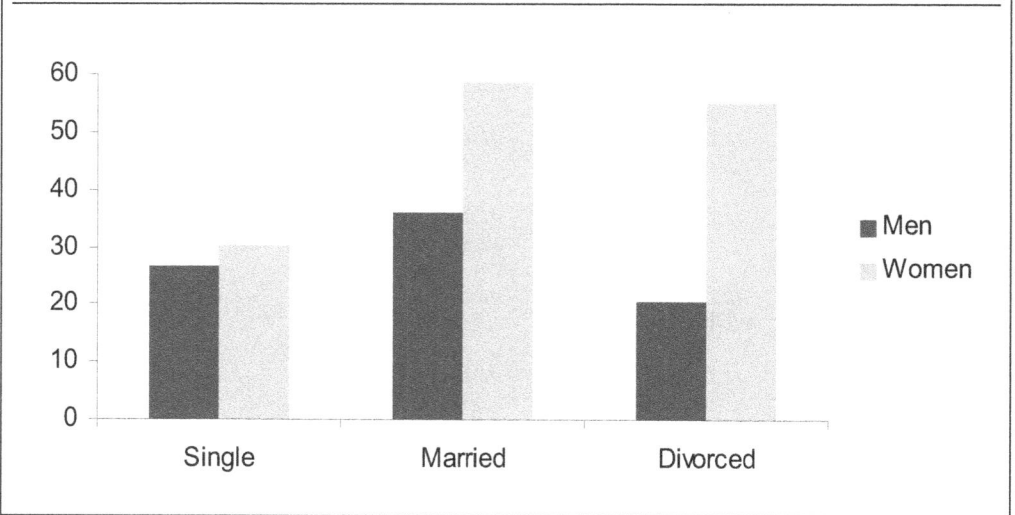

*Source:* Authors' calculations based on MECOVI (2005).

In addition, married women's employment outcomes are affected by their spouses' employment status. Women are more likely to be informal if the spouse works in the formal sector. This may reflect a tendency of women to reduce the intensity of their labor market participation when their spouse's labor income and benefits linked to formality—such as health insurance covering the whole family—increases. It could also be that women can afford the riskier status of informal work (in terms of, for example, job security and earnings variability) when the husband has a safer formal job, or that a husband with a regular formal job offers better access to capital for the wife's self-employment activity. Other studies show that the elasticity of women's working hours is negatively related to their spouse's wage variations (Mercado and Rios 2005), but further research is needed to verify the underlying causes for this relationship.

Family and home responsibilities also play a greater role in women's outcomes. As women move into their 30s, salaried employment—especially informal salaried employment—quickly falls in favor of self-employment (Figure 1.5). This coincides with growing family responsibilities. Male self-employment grows more slowly until the age of retirement, between 60 and 65. Men tend to turn to self-employment because they have accumulated the required financial and human capital to start their own enterprise or because they have been displaced by younger and better-educated workers. Retirement from formal and informal employment also favors self-employment because these individuals migrate to informal self-employment to continue generating income for their families in a more flexible sector. Figure 1.5 also captures cohort effects and the changes in gender roles reflected in the overall increase in female labor force participation in recent decades.

**Figure 1.5. Share of Informal Self-Employment in All Employment, by Age and Gender**

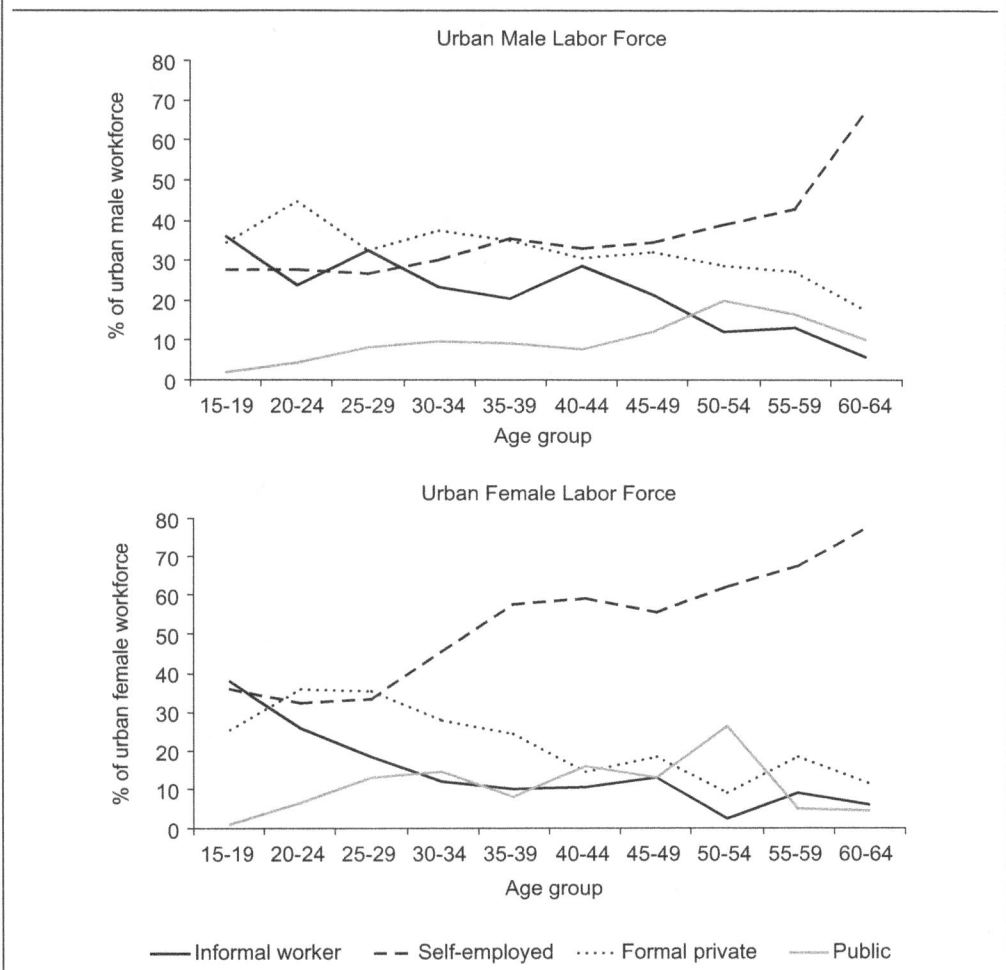

Urban Male Labor Force

Urban Female Labor Force

—— Informal worker    – – Self-employed    ····· Formal private    —— Public

*Source:* Authors' calculations based on MECOVI (2005).

Women concentrate in low-skill jobs, and the tendency toward higher informality rates among women is uniform across all sectors. In other words, occupational segregation by gender is stark. Women are concentrated in certain Low-skill activities include commerce, food, and domestic services. Men, on the other hand, are concentrated in manufacturing, construction, and transport employment (Figure 1.6).[2] Commerce employs one-third of women and just 15 percent of men, with informality rates of 95 percent and 75 percent, respectively. In manufacturing, the share of men and women holding jobs is similar (20 percent of men and 15 percent of women), but informality rates differ markedly (40 percent of men and 70 percent of women).

**Figure 1.6. Share of Informal Employment in All Employment, by Economic Sector and Gender, 2005**

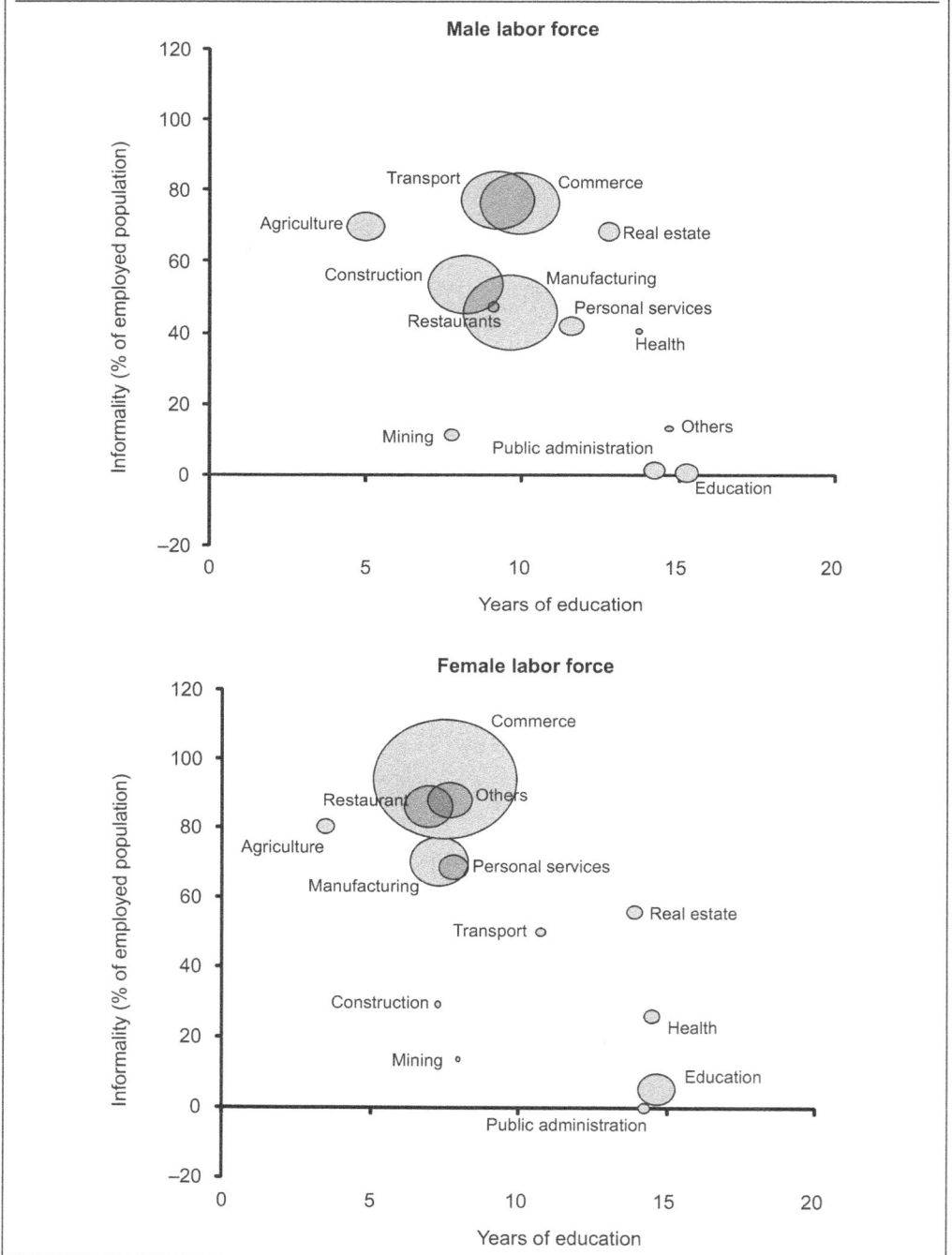

Male labor force

Female labor force

*Source*: World Bank (2007), based on MECOVI 2005.

*Note*: Bubbles represent the share of total population employed in each sector.

Women's lower educational achievement can help explain both higher rates of informality and concentration in low-productivity sectors and jobs. Figure 1.6 shows that average years of education of women are lower than men's, even when engaged in the same sectors. Long-standing gender gaps in education may thus help explain the concentration of women in certain low-productivity sectors and occupations. On average, workers in the informal sector have barely finished primary school—8.6 years of education on average, versus 12 years of schooling for formal employees. Three-quarters of workers without education engage in self-employment, compared with 60 percent for people with some education. While women have significantly lower educational attainment in the informal sector, this is not true in the formal sector; in fact, women have 0.7 more years of schooling than men employed in the private sector (Table 1.1).

**Table 1.1. Years of Schooling by Sector (Formal/Informal) and Gender**

|  | Informal Sector | | | Formal sector | | |
|---|---|---|---|---|---|---|
|  | Salaried | Self-employed | All | Public sector | Private sector | All |
| **Male** | 8.8 | 9.1 | 9.0 | 14.7 | 11.6 | 12.3 |
| **Female** | 7.7 | 7.1 | 7.3 | 13.8 | 12.3 | 12.8 |

*Source:* Authors' calculation based on MECOVI (2005).

Higher informality and lower educational achievement among women also affect gender-based wage gaps. Average income grows with the level of education and the level of formality. The hourly wages of women in the informal sector are lower than those of men, and women also have lower levels of education.[3] There are also severe gender wage gaps in the formal sector, particularly in the private sector. These discrepancies in wages, although mimicking regional trends, are more pronounced in Bolivia than Latin American country (LAC) averages.[4]

Protective labor regulation may create disincentives to hire women in the formal sector; however further analysis is needed to assess actual impact on labor force participation. Rigidities in labor regulations and high non-wage labor costs related to maternity leave and breastfeeding hours may discourage formal employers from hiring women (Box 1.1). Under current labor laws, women's employment in the formal sector is constrained by a shorter work week, night work prohibition, weak domestic work regulations (e.g., irregular work hours), and employer-paid maternity benefits that cannot be shared by husbands. At the same time, provisions against discrimination in remuneration and merit promotion are poorly enforced (World Bank 2005). Further research is needed to assess the impact of such gender-specific protective labor regulations on women's employment opportunities and labor force participation.

---

**Box 1.1. Rigidities in the Labor Market**

In Bolivia, non-wage labor costs amount to 13.7 percent of workers' wages and include 10 percent for sickness, maternity, and temporary disability benefits; 1.7 percent for permanent disability and survivor benefits; and 2 percent for housing (World Bank and IFC 2006). These costs approximate the regional average (12.5), although some countries—including Chile (3.4), El Salvador (8.9), Peru (9.8), and Uruguay (6.2)—have lower non-wages costs.

By regional standards, dismissals are severely constrained in Bolivia, firing costs are high, and vacations are long:

- The difficulty-of-firing index is at 100, the highest possible ranking, compared with 26.5 for LAC countries, because termination of workers owing to redundancy is not authorized, unlike most other LAC countries. Some countries—including Brazil, Costa Rica, and El Salvador—have no restrictions, while Chile only requires notifying the authorities.
- The difficulty-of-hiring index is well above the regional average because in Bolivia term contracts can be used only for term tasks, while in other countries—including Chile, Colombia, Ecuador, and Nicaragua—this restriction does not exist. Moreover, while term contracts are limited to three years in Bolivia, such other countries as Colombia, Cost Rica, El Salvador, and Mexico impose no time limits.
- A formal employer in Bolivia must pay the equivalent of 100 weeks of salary to dismiss a worker—one of the highest firing costs in the region. Moreover, an employer in Bolivia is required to give 90 days notice before a redundancy termination, and the penalty for a redundancy dismissal for workers with 20 years of service equals 21 months of wages.
- The rigidity-of-work-hour's index is high, mainly because vacations are long relative to regional standards: a Bolivian employee with 20 years of service has 30 days of paid vacation. This compares with 20 days in Mexico, 18 in Chile, 15 in Colombia, 12 in Costa Rica, and 11 in El Salvador. Furthermore, women have a shorter work week and are prohibited from night work.

*Source:* Policies for Increasing Firms' Formality and Productivity (World Bank 2007a) and World Bank (2005).

---

## Ethnicity, Education, and Informality: Compound Effects

The highest concentration of informal employment—especially self-employment—is found among indigenous women. More than 60 percent of the indigenous female labor force is engaged in informal self-employment, compared with fewer than 40 percent of the indigenous male labor force and the non-indigenous female labor force (Figure 1.7). Only 28 percent of the non-indigenous male labor force is self-employed.

Self-employed indigenous women face the largest wage gap relative to their non-indigenous and male peers. The ethnic wage gap is highest for self-employed indigenous women: these women earn just 60 percent of what non-indigenous women earn (Table 1.2). Indeed, a non-indigenous, self-employed woman earns 7.08 Bs an hour, compared with an hourly wage of only 4.23 Bs for self-employed indigenous women. (Self-employed indigenous men earn 6.30 Bs and non-indigenous men earn 7.48 Bs) But the gender wage gap virtually disappears when comparing non-indigenous men and women (men earn just 0.40 Bs more an hour than women); while it remains stark among indigenous workers (men earn 2.07 Bs more an hour than women). A study of changes in the relative earnings of the indigenous compared to the non-indigenous shows that indigenous earnings have declined in Bolivia over time (Tzannatos 2004), while indigenous men have enjoyed consistent gains in their earnings relative to women.

## Figure 1.7. Employment Outcomes by Gender and Ethnicity

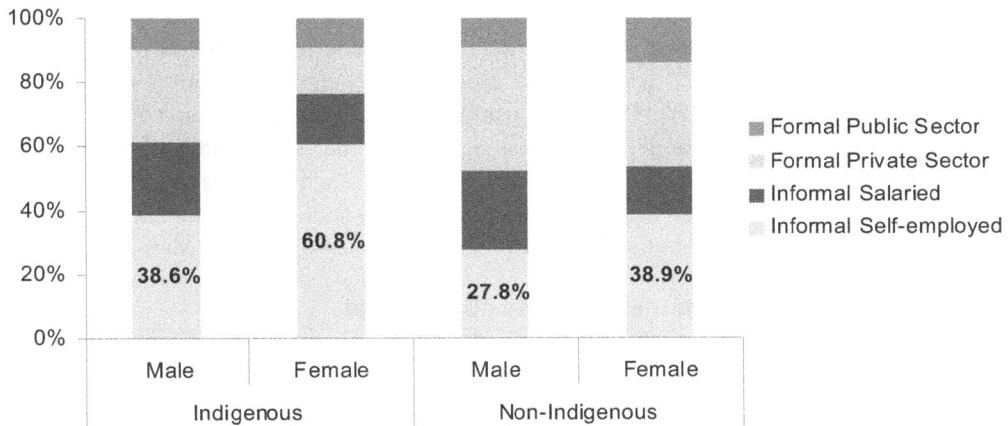

*Source:* Authors' calculation based on MECOVI (2005).

## Table 1.2. Gender and Ethnic Wage Gaps, by Employment Category

| | Gender wage gap (female wage as share of male, %) | | Ethnic wage gap (indigenous wage as share of non-indigenous, %) | |
|---|---|---|---|---|
| | Non-indigenous | Indigenous | Male | Female |
| Informal salaried | 71 | 62 | 86 | 76 |
| Informal self-employed | 95 | 67 | 84 | 60 |
| Formal public sector | 75 | 89 | 85 | 85 |
| Formal private sector | 79 | 67 | 78 | 67 |

*Source:* Authors' calculation based on MECOVI (2005).

Indigenous women's higher rates of informality and lower earnings mostly reflect the compound effects of ethnic and gender-based gaps in education.[5] Gender gaps in education are large, especially among the indigenous (Table 1.3). Self-employed indigenous men have on average 2.2 years of schooling more than self-employed indigenous women. And indigenous women lag behind their non-indigenous female peers; non-indigenous, self-employed women have on average 2.1 years more schooling than similarly engaged indigenous women.

## Table 1.3. Gender and Ethnic Education Gaps, by Employment Category

| | Gender education gap (years of schooling less for women) | | Ethnic education gap (years of schooling less for indigenous) | |
|---|---|---|---|---|
| | Non-indigenous | Indigenous | Male | Female |
| Informal salaried | 0.4 | 1.7 | 0.1 | 1.4 |
| Informal self-employed | 1.5 | 2.2 | 1.4 | 2.1 |
| Formal public sector | −0.8 | −0.2 | 1.3 | 1.9 |
| Formal private sector | 0.6 | 1.6 | 1.0 | 2.0 |

*Source:* Authors' calculation based on MECOVI (2005).

The precarious employment and earnings of indigenous women in Bolivia confirm regional trends. Evidence from other LAC countries confirms that economic opportunities are fewer and socioeconomic outcomes far worse among the indigenous and black populations when compared with national averages (Hall and Patrinos 2006, Patrinos and others 2007). Within these groups however, women often suffer greater levels of exclusion, which highlights the "cumulative disadvantages" based on both gender and race/ethnicity. This is in line with other studies that show indigenous and Afro-descendent women being excluded from jobs for women because of their race and excluded from jobs for men because they are women, as well as discrimination in terms of pay for being both indigenous and female (Crenshaw 2000, Buvinic and Mazza 2005).

## Why Gender Matters in the Bolivian Labor Market

We now provide a more in-depth analysis of gender differences in labor markets. Our analysis confirms that women, and especially indigenous women, fare significantly worse than men in terms of job quality and earnings. It also describes in further detail how women's employment and earnings are closely associated with lower educational attainment.

---

**Box 1.2. Benefits of Women Generating Income and Controlling Resources**

The 2007 Global Monitoring Report discusses the impacts of women's economic empowerment and concludes that "*the higher the share of household income and assets the mother controls, the higher the share of expenditure on health, nutrition and education and the lower the share spent on for instance cigarettes and alcohol.*" Needless to say, an increased earning capacity for women affects income levels and control, while also shifting patterns of spending in favor of areas that may help break the cycle of poverty (e.g., the health and education of children).

Evidence of this abounds. Studies in several African economies have shown that an increase in the share of women's assets and cash income boosts household spending on food and children's schooling and reduces spending by men on such items as alcohol and cigarettes (Levine, Ruel, and Morris 1999; Doss 2005; Hoddinott and Haddad 1995). In Ghana, in years when the production of women's crops is higher, the household spends a larger share of its budget on food and on private goods for women; in years when the production of men's crops is higher, the household spends more on goods consumed by men (Duflo and Udry 2004).

Other studies show that when women control more money, all measures of household welfare improve. In both Malawi and Bangladesh, when women are the direct beneficiaries of credit rather than men, the impact of credit on various measures of household welfare is greater (Diagne and others 2000). Pitt and Khandker (1998) find that female borrowing in micro-credit programs has a larger impact on children's school enrollment than male borrowing, while Duflo (2003) shows that girls who live with a grandmother eligible to receive pension benefits are healthier than those who live with a grandmother not eligible for such benefits. In contrast, the effects were not statistically significant for households in which the pension was received by a man. Thomas (1990) found that family health outcomes in Brazil, such as child survival probabilities, are improved much more by increases in mothers' as opposed to fathers' unearned income. Handa (1996) shows that in Jamaica, the presence in a household of a female decision-maker generally increases the share of the household budget allocated to child and family goods.

*Source*: Global Monitoring Report (World Bank 2007b).

Increasing the productivity and income of self-employed women is a worthy goal and is also a potentially powerful tool in Bolivia's efforts to reduce poverty. Increased income in the hands of women is likely to also contribute to the country's overall economic growth and poverty reduction. International evidence shows that raising the income-earning capacity of women has developmental impacts over and above its effects on household income, especially in terms of children's health and education and other measures of household welfare (Box 1.2). At the same time, even when controlling for differences in education and experience, Bolivian women on average earn 20–30 percent less than men (Andersen and Muriel 2002).

## Notes

[1] World Bank Gender Stats.

[2] Policies for Increasing Firms' Formality and Productivity (World Bank 2007a).

[3] Policies for Increasing Firms' Formality and Productivity (World Bank 2007a).

[4] A recent assessment of poverty in Bolivia finds that the employment gap faced by women and the earnings disparities solely related to gender are above regional averages (World Bank 2005).

[5] In terms of school enrollment and attendance, Quechua speakers are doing especially poorly while Aymaras do slightly better (World Bank 2006).

# CHAPTER 2

# Gender, Formality, and Profitability

Chapter 1 showed that women have higher participation rates than men in the informal sector, and in particular in informal self-employment. In fact, the majority of women in the Bolivian labor market (55 percent) run their own, informal businesses. This chapter focuses on self-employed men and women—that is, male and female-owned micro and small firms—and uses quantitative data from a survey of some 640 micro and small enterprise carried out in 2007 to investigate gender-based differences in the formality of firms and how it affects profitability; and the profitability of firms. The firm survey includes businesses from six sectors including: camelid products (alpaca and other types of wool), small commerce (grocery stores), food vendors (street vendors, small food stands, and restaurants), textiles (clothing manufacturing), wood products, and transport.[1] The definition of informality is again based on the registration of firms with tax authorities. Informal firms are those without a Tax Registration Number (NIT).

## Gender-Based Differences in the Formality of Businesses

Regardless of how informality is measured, female enterprise owners are less likely than male owners to run formalized operations. Fewer female-firm owners have registered for a municipal license (47 percent versus 61 percent of male firm owners) and only 22 percent of women in the firm survey sample had a tax number compared with 33 percent of men. In addition, only 1.6 percent of female-firm owners are registered with FundEmpresa, as against 8.3 percent of male owners. The higher tendency of women toward informality holds also when comparing firms of similar size (Table 2.1). Only when businesses have more than 11 employees are women's firms more formal than men's (World Bank 2007).

The different characteristics of male and female firm owners and the operations they run explain the lower levels of formality among female-owned businesses. Regression results (Appendixes 1 and 2) suggest that women are less involved in the formal sector because of differences in firm and owner characteristics. These include differences in motivation for entering self-employment; differences in self-efficacy[2] (women in the sample have lower entrepreneurial ability than men); differences in

**Table 2.1. Formality by Gender of Owner and Firm Size (%)**

|  | Number of Employees | Registered, FundEmpresa | Tax Number (NIT) | Municipal License |
|---|---|---|---|---|
| Female-owned firms | 0 | — | 7.5 | 34.0 |
|  | 1–4 | — | 10.8 | 38.9 |
|  | 5–10 | 4.3 | 52.9 | 71.0 |
|  | >11 | 28.6 | 100.0 | 100.0 |
|  | Total | 1.6 | 21.6 | 46.6 |
| Male-owned firms | 0 | — | — | 29.6 |
|  | 1–4 | 5.0 | 22.9 | 57.0 |
|  | 5–10 | 9.5 | 54.1 | 73.0 |
|  | >11 | 34.5 | 72.4 | 79.3 |
|  | Total | 8.4 | 33.0 | 60.5 |

*Source*: World Bank (2007a), World Bank Micro Enterprises Survey, 2007.

the size of the firm; and differences in the industries in which men and women are more concentrated. While more educated individuals are more likely to be in the formal sector, the ability of the owner and reasons for being in business matter more than education alone for determining the choice to become formal.

Controlling for these differences, men and women respond similarly to incentives to formalize. Estimates of a probit equation examining determinants of formality separately for men and women suggest that men and women formalize their businesses for similar reasons once controlled for difference in firms and owner characteristics (Appendixes 1 and 2). The top three motivations to formalize for both men and women are (Table 2.2) to obey the law, increase their client base, and avoid fines. The only difference between men and women is found among businesses with municipal licenses; here, women more often cite obeying the law while men are more concerned with avoiding fines.

**Table 2.2. Percentage of Respondents Who Formalized their Businesses to...**

|  | Firms with NIT | | | Firms with Municipal License | | |
|---|---|---|---|---|---|---|
|  | Total | Male | Female | Total | Male | Female |
| Obey the law | 48 | 46 | 47 | 58 | 44 | 52 |
| Increase client base | 26 | 24 | 25 | 6 | 10 | 8 |
| Avoid fines | 16 | 21 | 18 | 25 | 34 | 29 |
| Reduce bribes | 2 | 1 | 2 | 4 | 5 | 5 |
| Gain access to credit | 4 | 0 | 2 | 3 | 1 | 2 |
| No benefit or don't know | 5 | 9 | 7 | 4 | 6 | 5 |

*Source*: Authors' own calculations based on World Bank Micro Enterprises Survey (2007).

The impact of formality on profitability[3] depends on the size of the firm, regardless of the firm owner's gender. To examine the effect of firm size on formality and, thus, on profitability, the companion study (World Bank 2007) arrives at propensity-score-matching estimates of the effect of a tax number according to firm size (Appendix 1). The results (Figure 2.1) show that the benefits of holding a tax number are greatest for mid-size firms—those with capital stock between 8,000 Bs and 34,000 Bs and between three and five workers. For those firms, formality increased the profitability of the firms by up to 36 percent. In contrast, formality *decreased* the profitability of micro firms (with capital of less than 8,000 Bs and less than three workers) and larger firms (with capital of greater than 34,000 Bs and more than five workers) by 22 percent (Figure 2.1). Propensity-score-matching estimates by gender show that point estimates for female-owned businesses are generally in line with the pooled results for men and women. The results suggest that the value of a tax enrollment number (NIT) is negative for female-owned firms with one or fewer workers, but positive for those with between two and five workers. The sample of female-owned firms with more than six workers is too small (11 observations) to generate meaningful estimates.

The nonlinear relationship between formality and profitability is explained by how firms of different size deal with different costs and benefits of becoming formal. The smallest firms may not benefit from becoming formal because of the immediate rise in costs, while benefits in terms of an increased customer base or better access to credit remain difficult to realize given the small size of these firms' operations. The companion study also shows that the main benefit of getting an NIT appears to be the ability to expand the customer base by issuing tax receipts. For small firms interested in growing, the cost of formalizing then is offset by the benefits awaiting them as they become slightly bigger. As a reflection of this, the companion report finds that firm owners who formalize when small tend to also be those with greater entrepreneurial skills and more developed business growth plans.

**Figure 2.1 Average Impact of Having a Tax Number on Profitability, by Firm Size**

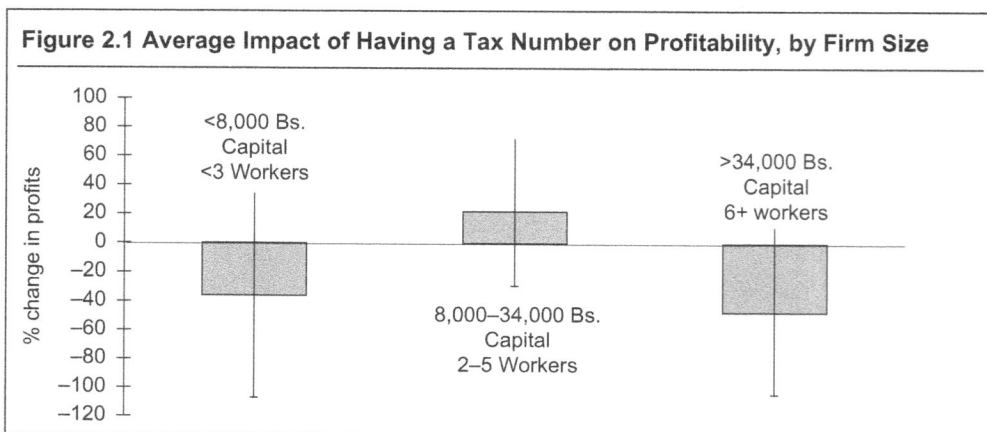

*Source*: World Bank (2007a) based on World Bank Micro Enterprises Survey 2007.
*Note*: Bars show point estimates from Propensity Score Matching. Lines show 95 percent confidence intervals.

The profitability of larger informal firms is negatively affected by registering with the tax authorities. Larger informal firms tend to have owners with less formal education, but higher entrepreneurial ability than firms of the same size with an NIT. Larger informal firms have similar access to loans, and working capital, from banks or other financial institutions as formal firms their size. Thus, for a firm that has managed to attain this size while staying informal, the main impact of getting an NIT is just higher taxes. Most (71 percent) of these larger informal firms, while not registered with tax authorities, have a municipal license. This may allow them to appear formal to the municipal authorities, and possibly to financial institutions.

## Gender-Based Differences in Profitability

Female firm owners earn significantly lower profits than their male counterparts, regardless of formality status. Monthly profits of male-owned firms are 1.7 times larger than those of female-owned firms (Figure 2.2). The mean monthly profit for female owners in 2005 was 962 Bs, compared with 1,605 Bs for male owners. Owing to small sample sizes when disaggregating by gender and sector, we only report findings for three out of the six sectors. Similar gender gaps are found in food sales and textiles. In contrast, the profits of male owners of grocery stores are about 14 percent less a month than female owners. The greatest gender gap is found in textiles, where the profits of male-run operations are nearly three times as high as female-run operations.

**Figure 2.2. Gender Gaps in Mean Monthly Profits, by Sector (Male Profits as a Share of Female Profits)**

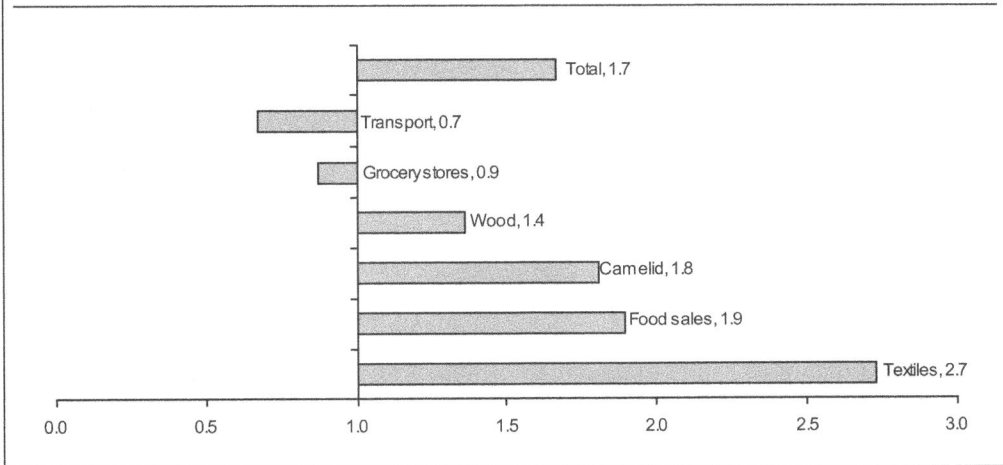

Source: Authors' calculations based on World Bank Micro Enterprises Survey 2007.
Note: There are only six observations of male owners in the camelid sector, three observations of female owners in transportation, and nine observations of female owners in wood products.

**Figure 2.3. Gender Gaps in Hourly Wages, by Sector
(Male Hourly Wage as a Share of Female Hourly Wage)**

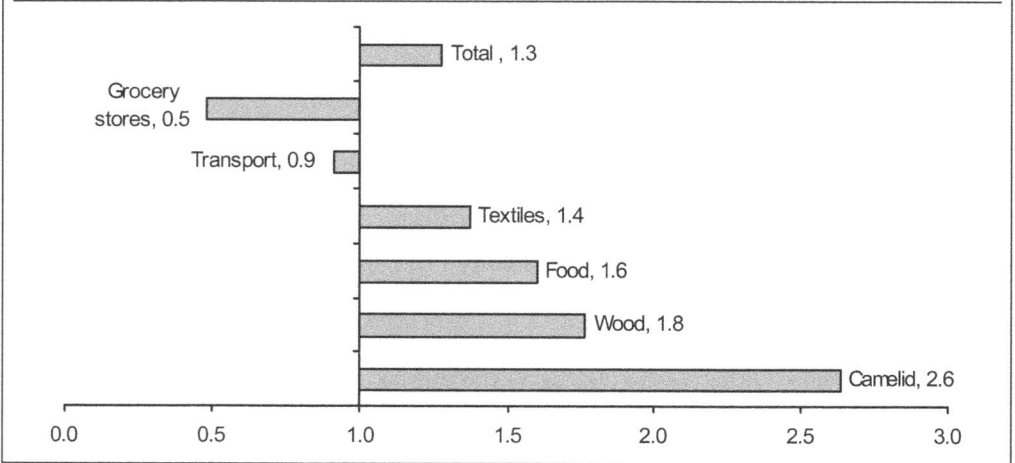

Source: Authors' calculations based on World Bank Micro Enterprises Survey 2007.
Note: There are only six observations of male owners in the camelid sector, three observations of female owners in transportation, and nine observations of female owners in wood products.

After controlling for hours worked, male owners still earn higher profits than female owners. Male owners report working on average 62 hours a week, versus 58 hours for women. Male owners' hourly income—calculated as monthly profits divided by hours worked each month—averages 30 percent above that of their female peers (Figure 2.3). On average, female firm owners earn 6.5 Bs an hour compared with 8.3 Bs for men. The greatest differences are found in the wood and camelid sectors, however the number of observations when slicing the data by gender and sectors is too low in these two sectors for the estimates to be significant. As food vendors or owners of small restaurants, men earn 60 percent more than women. The only sector in which women do better than men is grocery stores where they earn about twice as much an hour as men.

Gender gaps in education and experience explain only about one sixth of the profitability gap between men and women. To understand the underlying causes, we used Ordinary Least Squares (OLS) regression analysis to decompose the gender gap in hourly profits. We included only firms that are fully owned by the owner-manager's family. We have adequate information to carry out a regression analysis for about 446 firms, of which half are managed by women. The OLS estimates suggests the following (Table 2.3):

## Table 2.3. Earnings (Hourly Profits) OLS Regressions for Small and Micro Businesses

| Explanatory variables | (1) ln(Hourly wage) | | (2) ln(Hourly wage) | | (3) ln(Hourly wage) | | (4) in(Hourly wage) | | (5) ln(Hourly wage) | |
|---|---|---|---|---|---|---|---|---|---|---|
| Woman (dummy) | −0.481 | *** | −0.404 | *** | −0.146 | — | 0.031 | — | 0.171 | — |
| Education (years) | | | 0.027 | ** | 0.015 | — | 0.024 | * | 0.019 | — |
| Experience (years) | | | 0.011 | * | 0.006 | — | 0.009 | — | 0.006 | — |
| ln(total assets) | | | | | 0.084 | *** | 0.072 | *** | 0.054 | ** |
| Number of employees | | | | | 0.100 | *** | 0.103 | *** | 0.101 | *** |
| Sector dummies | | | | | | | | | | |
| - Transport | | | | | | | −0.075 | — | −0.089 | — |
| - Grocery stores | | | | | | | −0.896 | *** | −0.908 | *** |
| - Food sales | | | | | | | 0.211 | — | 0.233 | — |
| - Wood products | | | | | | | 0.001 | — | −0.002 | — |
| - Camelid products | | | | | | | −0.454 | ** | −0.020 | — |
| Bank loans | | | | | | | | | 0.272 | ** |
| Micro credit | | | | | | | | | 0.066 | — |
| NIT | | | | | | | | | 0.046 | — |
| Export | | | | | | | | | −0.473 | — |
| Share female employees | | | | | | | | | −0.351 | — |
| Indigenous owner | | | | | | | | | 0.152 | — |
| Single woman | | | | | | | | | 0.205 | — |
| Keeps accounts | | | | | | | | | 0.103 | — |
| Location dummies | | | | | | | | | | |
| - Urban | | | | | | | | | 0.705 | ** |
| - Santa Cruz | | | | | | | | | −0.077 | — |
| - Cochabamba | | | | | | | | | −0.181 | — |
| - El Alto | | | | | | | | | −0.459 | *** |
| Constant | 1.429 | *** | 0.999 | *** | 0.449 | ** | 0.556 | ** | 0.172 | — |
| Number of obs. | 450 | | 444 | | 444 | | 444 | | 440 | |
| $R^2$ | 0.0353 | | 0.0462 | | 0.1416 | | 0.2180 | | 0.2607 | |

*Source*: World Bank Micro Enterprises Survey 2007.

*Notes*: Sample includes only businesses with less than 25 employees, entirely owned by the respondent from the World Bank Micro Enterprises Survey 2007.

*** Significant at the 1 percent level, ** Significant at the 5 percent level, * Significant at the 10 percent level, — Not significant.

- Women earn on average 38 percent smaller profits than men, after accounting for hours worked (Column 1).[4]
- Controlling for education and experience, the gender gap is reduced slightly but women still earn 33 percent less than men (Column 2).
- Controlling for size (in the form of productive capital[5] and number of employees), the gender gap becomes statistically insignificant (Column 3). In other words, the 33 percent gender gap calculated after controlling for

education and experience can be entirely explained by differences in productive capital.

▪ Adding dummies for sectors of operation causes the gender gap to turn positive, in favor of women, but statistically indifferent from 0 (Column 4). This reflects the fact that women tend to choose sectors with relatively low levels of returns, such as grocery stores, camelid, and textiles (food sales, however, is a relatively attractive sector).

▪ As already suggested by other studies, having a tax number (i.e., being formalized) does not affect gender gaps in profitability.

Further analysis provides no evidence of gender-based differences in the impact of formality on profitability, and the lower profits of female-owned firms are fully explained by differences in scale and sector of operation, as well as owner characteristics (related to education and experience). The estimated results of a probit equation examining the impact of having an NIT tax registration number and other characteristics on profitability do not mean that formality has the same impact on male-owned businesses as it does on female-owned businesses (Appendixes 1 and 3). Moreover, the results do not exclude the possibility that the production function for profits is the same for men and women. Regression results suggest that women perform worse because of differences from male business owners in the sector and scale of operations, in motivations for entering self-employment, and in entrepreneurial ability.

## Why Female-Owned Firms Are More Informal and Less Profitable

The main variables contributing to lower profitability and higher informality among female-owned businesses are related to different reasons for being in business, the lower education and ability (self-efficacy) of women, the smaller size of female-owned firms, and the concentration of female-owned firms in low-profitability sectors.

### Differences in Reasons for Becoming Self-Employed

The need to care for the family is both the main reason women enter into self-employment and a constraint to increasing the productivity of their firms. As discussed in Chapter 1, women may be seeking informal and self-employment because they want greater flexibility to balance home and work responsibilities. In the firm survey, 73 percent of married female owners said that the ability to care for family members is a critical reason for becoming self-employed, compared with only 45 percent of married men. Likewise, nearly 70 percent of married women are looking mainly for flexible work hours while only 45 percent married men are (Figure 2.4). The most important motivations of single women were to be independent (82 percent) and to expand their businesses (76 percent).

**Figure 2.4. Reasons for Preferring Self-Employment, Married Men and Women (% that Responded "Very Important")**

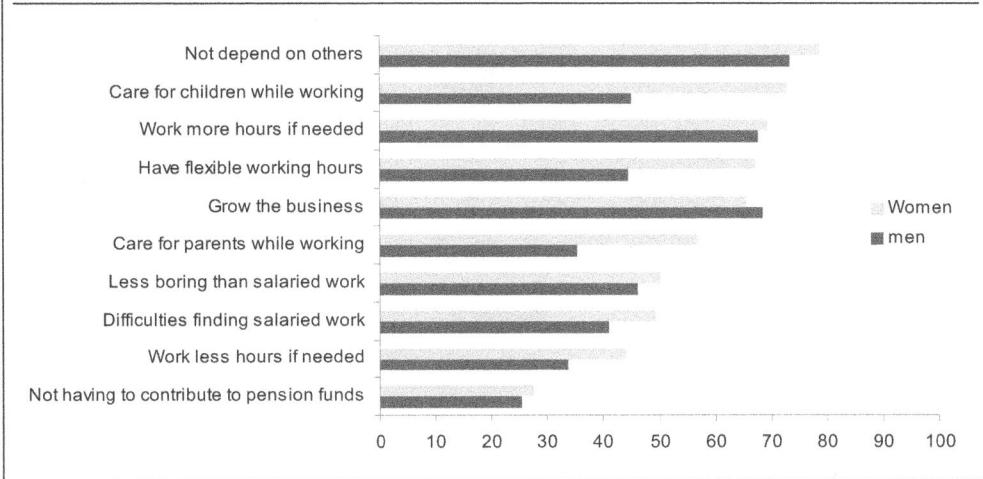

*Source*: Authors' own calculations based on World Bank Micro Enterprises Survey 2007.

Furthermore, motivations for entering self-employment relate to the marital status and age (life cycle) of female firm owners. Chapter 1 showed how differences in employment outcomes across men and women's life cycle reflect the greater role of family and home responsibilities for women's outcomes. Women are far more inclined than men to say that they entered self-employment to complement family income after the age of 19—roughly 60 percent versus some 15 percent for men. Similarly, about 25 percent of women over the age of 19 say they entered self-employment to care for the home, while no men did. Studying the flow of people between formal and informal employment in Argentina, Brazil, and Mexico, Perry and others (2007) find unusually dynamic mobility for women—most of them married—moving between the labor force and informal self-employment. The authors conclude that this group of self-employed women is probably most concerned with supplementing family income rather than developing a business.

*Lower Educational Achievement*

Female firm owners have on average much lower educational levels than their male counterparts, although with differences across sectors. Male firm owners have on average 2.2 more years of schooling than women (Figure 2.5). The gender gap in education differs depending on sector, but even in the sector with the lowest gender gap, male owners have nearly two years more schooling than female owners, The largest gender gap in education is found in the food sales sector, where male owners have on average 4.2 years more schooling than women.

**Figure 2.5. Gender Gaps in Years of Schooling, by Sector
(Years of Schooling for Men Less Years of Schooling for Women)**

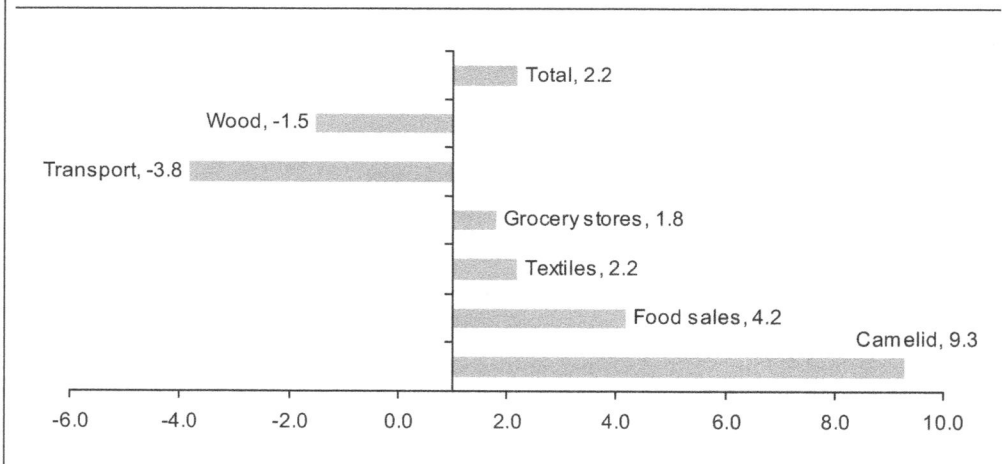

*Source*: Authors' own calculations based on World Bank Micro Enterprises Survey, 2007.
*Note*: There are only six observations of male owners in the camelid sector, three observations of female owners in transportation, and nine observations of female owners in wood products.

*Smaller Scale of Operations*

Female-owned operations are far smaller in scale than male-owned operations. On average, male-owned businesses have three times the assets of female-owned businesses and employ an average of 3.5 people, compared with 2.7 people for female-owned businesses (Table 2.4). Sectoral differences are significant. Gender gaps are particularly pronounced in textiles, where men have 5.4 employees and productive assets of 46,642 Bs on average, while women operate with two employees and productive assets of only 7,267 Bs.

**Table 2.4. Scale of Operations as Measured by Assets
and Number of Employees, by Gender**

|  |  | Total All Sectors | Textiles | Groceries | Food Sales |
|---|---|---|---|---|---|
| Assets [a] (Bs) | Men | 64,690 | 46,642 | 13,099 | 16,715 |
|  | Women | 20,969 | 7,267 | 47,050 | 7,661 |
|  | Gender Gap [b] | 3.1 | 6.4 | 0.3 | 2.2 |
| Employees (number) | Men | 3.5 | 5.4 | 3.5 | 4.9 |
|  | Women | 2.7 | 2 | 2.8 | 2.6 |
|  | Gender Gap | 1.3 | 2.7 | 1.3 | 1.9 |

*Source*: Authors' own calculations based on World Bank Micro Enterprises Survey 2007.
*Notes*: a. Excludes real estate. b. Gender gaps are calculated as men's assets as a share of women's and the number of employees of male owners as a share of the number of employees of female owners.

**Figure 2.6 Distribution of Male and Female Sample, by Sector**

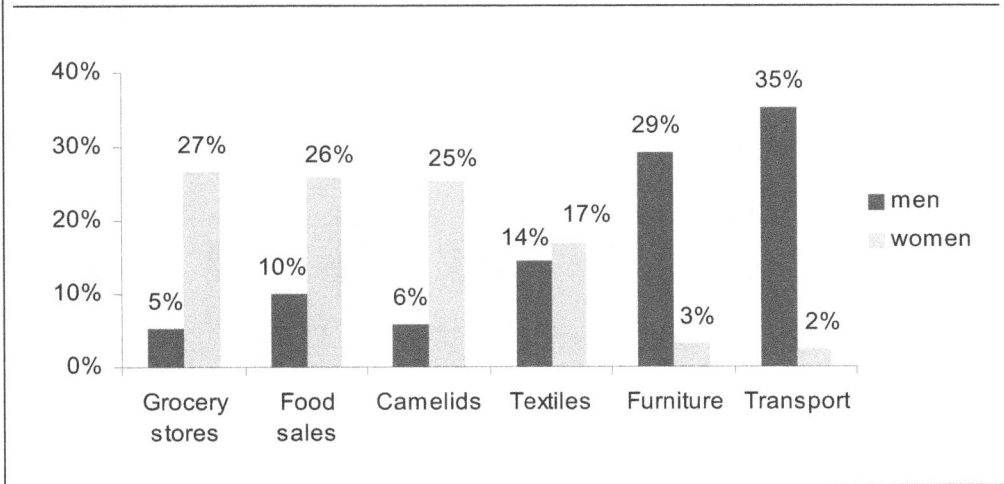

*Source*: Authors' calculations based on World Bank Micro Enterprises Survey, 2007.

Some female business owners operate on a smaller scale by choice. In some cases, women opt for a lower scale of operations so they can also tend to household duties. A larger scale of operations would negate some of the advantages to women of micro-businesses—including not having to depend on others, to be able to care for children simultaneously, and having flexible work hours. When women were asked what they considered the ideal number of employees for their business five years into the future, the average said is 6.9 employees; this compares with 9.2 cited by men.

*Concentration in Low-Profitability Sectors*

Female enterprises are concentrated in particular sectors. Ninety-five percent of female-owned businesses operate in four of the six sectors surveyed: grocery stores (27 percent), food vending (26 percent), camelid (25 percent), and textiles or clothing manufacturing (17 percent) (Figure 2.6). Conversely, 64 percent of male-owned businesses operate in the wood manufacturing and transport sectors, where the presence of female-owned firms is between 2 percent and 3 percent.

Female-owned firms are twice as likely to operate out of the home as male-owned businesses. Operating out of the home is associated with greater flexibility and also means a lower likelihood of visits from tax inspectors. At the same time, the greater tendency to operate out of the home also reflects the industry in which women work. Controlling for industry of work, females and males are equally likely to work at home. The sectoral composition of women's activities then clearly affects how female-owned businesses operate.

Women also operate in low-profitability sectors. The four sectors in which women concentrate are also the ones where women earn the lowest monthly profits (Figure 2.7). This is especially true for the camelid and textiles sectors, where monthly profits average only 651 Bs and 755 Bs, respectively.

**Figure 2.7. Monthly Profits, by Sector and Gender**

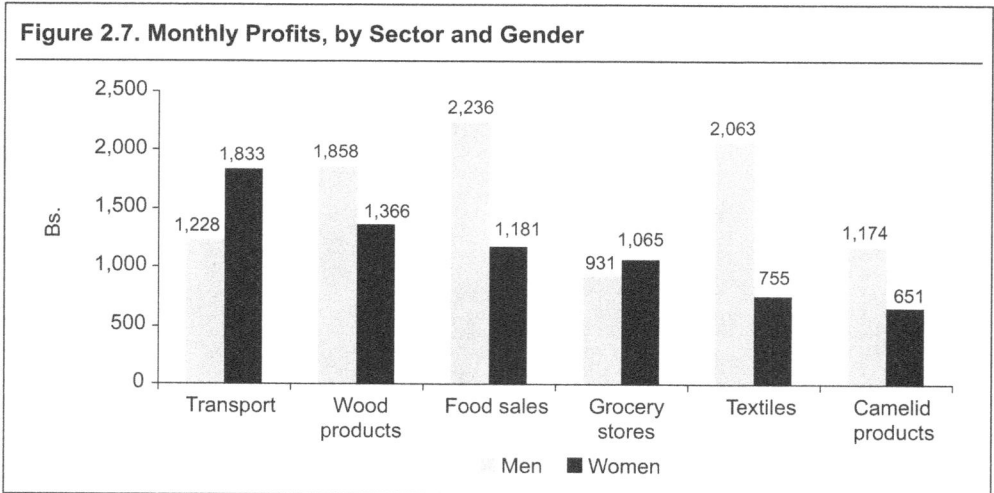

*Source*: Authors' own calculations based on World Bank Micro Enterprises Survey, 2007.
*Note*: There are only six observations of male owners in the camelid sector, three observations of female owners in transportation, and nine observations of female owners in wood products

Sector-specific characteristics (e.g., low-skilled, high levels of flexibility) may explain the concentration of women in the least profitable sectors:

- The food sales sector is dominated by women and requires relatively little investment and education, but yields *relatively* higher profits.
- Grocery stores are attractive to women despite the long working hours and low salary because they afford women independence (neither bosses nor employees) and women can simultaneously care for their home and children.
- The camelid product sector pays lower monthly profits than the other sectors, but women engaged in it have lower levels of education and dedicate much less time and capital to it. It is also commonly seen as complementing agricultural activities.
- The textiles sector is almost equally divided between male and female business owners, but women earn much less than men. Again, this is due to the much smaller scale of operations. Women, on average, work 19 hours less than men each week, invest less than half the capital, and have less than half the number of employees, so it is no surprise that their monthly profits are less than half those of men in the sector. However, the hourly wage is relatively high—Bs 7.5/hour, higher than for women in any other sector apart from food sales.

## Conclusions on Gender-Based Differences in Formality and Profitability

Female business owners are less likely than their male peers to run formalized operations, owing to differences in the characteristics of male and female owners and between male- and female-run operations. A key difference is the smaller scale of female-run operations, which is crucial because the productivity benefits of becoming formal depend on the size of the firm. Beyond differences in these characteristics, there is no evidence of gender-based differences in the determinants of becoming formal. Furthermore, male and female entrepreneurs that have formalized their operations cite the same reasons for doing so.

Women firm owners also earn significantly lower profits than their male counterparts, again owing to differences in the characteristics of male and female owners and between male- and female-owned operations. Regression analyses show that the differences in the profitability of male- and female-run businesses are mainly explained by differences in business size, and also affected by differences in sectors of operations and in the education and experience of owners. Once those factors are controlled for, the impact of informality on profitability become similar for male and female-owned firms.

## Notes

[1] We selected the six sectors to balance representativeness of the active population employed in the informal sector. Our firm selection seeks to ensure participation from a range of industries, from both formal and informal sectors, and from urban and rural areas. The selection therefore includes four of the top five industries for urban informality. Two of the additional sectors surveyed were wood and camelids because they are linked to the agriculture sector (representing most of rural informality); they allow for surveys in both urban and rural areas; and they engage in some export activity. In addition, they are among the priority sectors for strategic public investment (complejos productivos).

[2] Understood here as a combination of the ability and self-confidence needed to run a business; see de Mel, McKenzie, and Woodruff 2007.

[3] This analysis focuses on firm profitability, rather than firm productivity, for several reasons. First, profitability is the most important measure for firm owners when deciding whether to become formal, regardless of whether formality increases profits through greater productivity, access to better input prices, economies of scale, or other channels. Second, since a large share of business profits are withdrawn as income for the self-employed, profit is the measure of interest for considering poverty alleviation. Technically, measuring the productivity of enterprises can be very hard and yield misleading results (Katayama, Lu, and Tybout 2006). See also World Bank (2007).

[4] The coefficient of −0.481 on the gender dummy implies that women on average earn 38 percent less than men $(1 - \exp(-0.481))$

[5] The measure used is the log of productive capital, excluding buildings and land but including the replacement cost of inventory. The reasons for the exclusion of land and buildings are that: many firms operate out of their homes so the value of these assets are also capturing home use; since land and buildings don't appreciate, but are a source of investment in and of themselves, they typically earn lower returns to the business than equipment and inventories; and financing for equipment and inventories tends to differ from financing of buildings and land.

# CHAPTER 3

# Gender-Specific Constraints to Productivity

In this chapter, we examine a set of gender-specific productivity constraints faced by female owners of small and micro-firms, which limit the growth of their businesses. We first focus on variables that reduce women's access to productive assets, including financial, physical, and human capital. We then look at other factors that impede women's participation in economic activity, both in the marketplace and at home.

The analysis in this chapter is based on data from the micro and small enterprises survey, combined with qualitative data gathered during focus group discussions with women in four major cities in Bolivia. Twenty focus groups met in February and June 2007 and included self-employed women engaged primarily in four sectors (camelid, grocery stores, food vendors, and textiles). We discuss the methodological strengths and weaknesses of the data gathered in focus groups in Box 3.1.

---

**Box 3.1. Focus-Group Methodology and Working with Data Based on Perceptions**

---

To identify the constraints to higher productivity and formalization perceived by female firm owners in Bolivia's large informal sector, this study conducted eight focus group discussions in El Alto, La Paz, Cochabamba, and Santa Cruz with self-employed women in four sectors: grocery stores, restaurants and food sales, textiles (clothing manufacturing from wool and cloth), and camelid (clothing manufacturing from llama and alpaca wool).[1]

In addition to the focus group interviews, we use data from the 2006 Investment Climate Assessment (ICA) for Bolivia, as well as data from the 2007 micro-enterprise surveys of formal and informal firms. Analyzing qualitative data from the three sources offers a broad view of why firms entered their lines of business, the constraints they face to greater productivity and formalization, and what can be done to alleviate the constraints. The sample interviewed is not statistically representative of the focus group, but is representative of the ICA and the micro survey. But the focus group methodology uncovered new evidence about perceptions and helped reveal the reasons behind firms' behavior.

*(Box continues on next page)*

---

**Box 3.1 (continued)**

---

The main limitations of using data based on firms' perception of the constraints they face (as in the ICA or the micro survey) relate to four variables: to each individual firm's relative optimism or pessimism regarding its environment; how each firm understands each question, which, given differences in understanding, induces potentially excessive heterogeneity in responses; there is a reverse causality between the firms' own characteristics with regard to productivity and formality and what firms perceive as constraints—meaning, for example, that more productive firms tend to perceive fewer constraints; and the data do not always reflect the expected strong correlation between constraints and the consequences of those constraints for firms. For example, there should be a high correlation between firms that complain about corruption and how much or how often they have to pay bribes. All these limitations can be simply checked for in the data and addressed.

The main advantage of perception data is that people make decisions based on their perception of the opportunities and constraints they face. Furthermore, the data highlight how each constraint affects each firm's productivity. Hence, the perception of the constraint is directly linked to a practical implication for productivity rather than a vague statement. In light of these merits and limitations, comparative analysis of the constraints faced by informal versus formal firms, small versus micro firms, or firms in one sector versus those in another, for example, should yield a better understanding of productivity and formalization issues.

*Source*: World Bank (2007).

---

## Male and Female Views on Productivity Constraints

Male and female business owners, of both formal and informal firms, do not differ significantly in their ranking of productivity constraints. When questioned about the importance of various constraints, male and female business owners ranked the following highest: economy-wide constraints such as crime, corruption, and instability; sector-specific constraints linked to competition and market size; and barriers to accessing credit (Figure 3.1). More than half of both men and women in the sample felt that crime and corruption pose major constraints to productivity. Between 40 percent and 50 percent of both men and women identified the cost of credit and prerequisites needed to obtain credit as very important constraints to productivity. Similar shares were found for informal competition and market size.

The only constraints ranked as very important by a larger share of women than men were childcare and household chores. While one in four women felt that household chores were very important obstacles to productivity, only one in ten men did. And while 17 percent of women saw the need to care for children as an important constraint, only 8 percent of men did. Differences aside, the shares of both men and women concerned about these issues were low relative to other productivity constraints.

**Figure 3.1 Productivity Constraints by Gender
(% That Listed Issue as Very Important)**

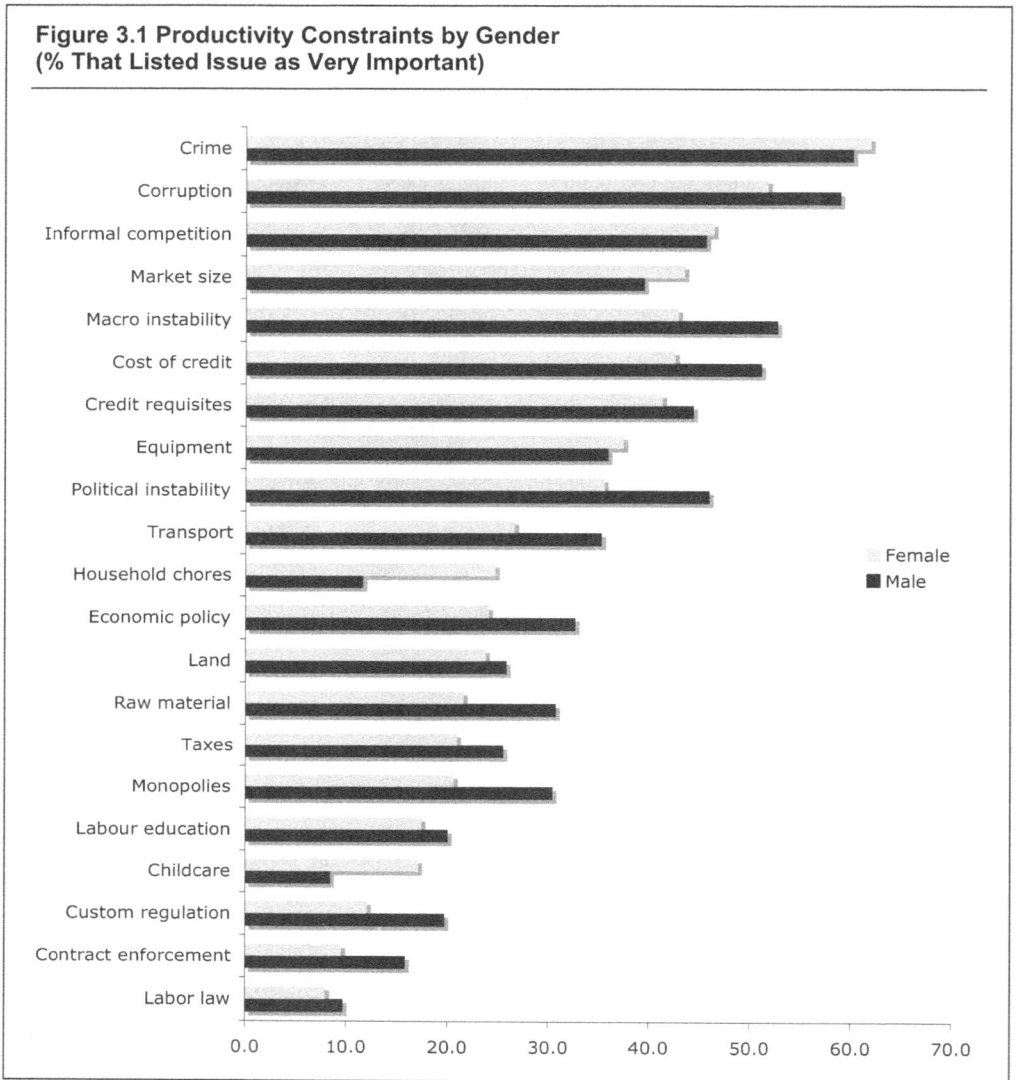

Legend:
- Female
- Male

Categories (top to bottom): Crime, Corruption, Informal competition, Market size, Macro instability, Cost of credit, Credit requisites, Equipment, Political instability, Transport, Household chores, Economic policy, Land, Raw material, Taxes, Monopolies, Labour education, Childcare, Custom regulation, Contract enforcement, Labor law

X-axis: 0.0  10.0  20.0  30.0  40.0  50.0  60.0  70.0

*Source*: Authors own calculations based on World Bank Micro Enterprises Survey, 2007.

## Gender-Based Constraints in Access to Productive Assets

While male and female business owners agree on many of the same constraints to productivity, the mechanisms through which these constraints manifest themselves may differ. In the following discussion of access to finance—a constraint ranked high by both men and women—we illustrate this. We then discuss gender-based constraints in physical, social, and human capital.

Figure 3.2. Bank Loan and Micro Credit, by Gender

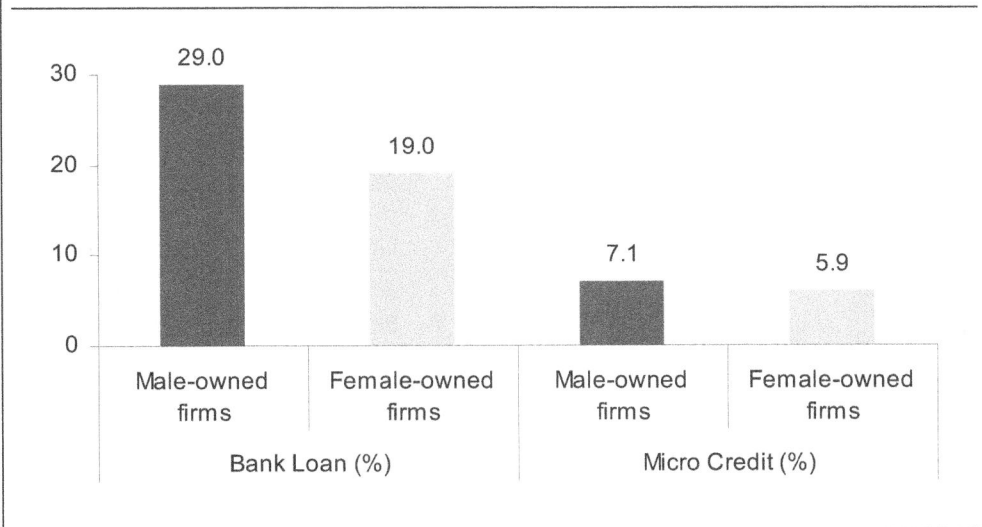

Source: Authors' own calculations based on World Bank Micro Enterprises Survey, 2007.

### Access to Finance for Female-Owned Businesses

Female-owned businesses rely less on formal financing mechanisms than male-owned businesses. In Bolivia, female owners of micro and small firms are less likely to resort to the formal banking sector—just 19 percent have bank loans, versus 29 percent of male owners (Figure 3.2). Even looking at micro credit—a sector dominated by institutions that target women—male business owners are still slightly more likely to obtain credit (7 percent) than women (6 percent).

Gender differences in the reliance on formal versus informal sources of finance are particularly glaring at low scales of operations. The major sources of financing for female firm owners, especially at lower scales of operations, are savings, family and friends, and rotational saving schemes known as *pasanaku* (Table 3.1). In firms with one–four employees, only 20 percent of women business owners receive bank credit for business start-ups compared with 29 percent for men, and only 23 percent of female business owners have credit from a financial institution, versus 36 percent of male owners. Reliance on informal saving mechanisms (*pasanaku*) is also significantly higher among women, while men are more likely to operate with a formal savings account. Excessive reliance on informal lending by female-headed micro enterprises is seen as indicative of gender-specific market constraints in formal credit in similar studies from other Latin America countries (e.g., Pagan and Sánchez 2001 for Mexico). This has economic costs as growth may be stunted when firms rely only on internal or informal sources of financing (Ayyagari and others 2006).

**Table 3.1. Use of Financial Services, by Gender and Firm Size**

| | Number of employees | Bank credit for start-up | Working capital from banks | Savings account | Loan from financial institution | Pasanaku[a] |
|---|---|---|---|---|---|---|
| **Female-owned firms** | 0 | 13.2 | 1.9 | 7.5 | 13.2 | 17.0 |
| | 1–4 | 20.0 | 5.9 | 14.1 | 22.7 | 23.8 |
| | 5–10 | 32.9 | 11.4 | 33.3 | 40.0 | 25.7 |
| | >11 | 28.6 | 14.3 | 71.4 | 42.9 | 14.3 |
| | Total | 21.9 | 6.7 | 18.5 | 25.4 | 22.9 |
| **Male-owned firms** | 0 | 22.2 | 3.7 | 18.5 | 11.1 | 11.1 |
| | 1–4 | 29.1 | 6.7 | 27.9 | 35.8 | 10.1 |
| | 5–10 | 31.1 | 9.5 | 44.6 | 35.1 | 10.8 |
| | >11 | 31.0 | 13.8 | 67.9 | 44.8 | 17.2 |
| | Total | 29.1 | 7.8 | 34.7 | 34.3 | 11.0 |

*Source*: Authors' own calculations based on World Bank Micro Enterprises Survey, 2007.
*Note:* a *Pasanaku* refers to informal rotating savings and credit associations.

Most women operate at lower scales of operation where gender-based differences in access to financial services are the greatest. Ninety-five percent of female business owners work in the four sectors (textiles, food, camelid, and grocery stores) where the average size of female-run businesses is between two and three employees. In other words, gender-based differences in the use of financial services are greater at the scales where most female-owned businesses operate, reducing women's ability to increase productivity and expand their businesses.

Gender gaps in the use of financial services narrow with firm size and all but disappear as firms grow beyond a certain size. The use of credit and other financial services increases with firm size, regardless of owner gender. Once businesses employ five or more employees, female-owned businesses seem to have equal and in some cases better access to credit than male-owned businesses (Table 3.1). At this scale of operations, nearly 29 percent of female-owned businesses have bank credit for start-up, as against 31 percent of men, while more women than men receive bank-financed working capital or loans from financial institutions.

That female-run businesses rely less on financial services, especially formal ones, owes primarily to such demand-side constraints as low levels of education and a strong aversion to credit. Lower levels of education, financial literacy, and managerial skills make it harder for women to apply for business loans. Female business owners experience bureaucratic procedures as a powerful deterrent to applying for a loan (Box 3.2). Because of the informal nature of women's work and their lower levels of education, self-employed women are also less likely to produce, maintain, and provide proper documentation (e.g., audited statements, government registration, licenses, or business plans) to secure a loan. The qualitative data also suggest that female firm owners harbor strong aversions to obtaining credit.

**Box 3.2. Female Small and Micro-Firm Owners' Perceptions of Constraints to Accessing Finance**

The principle obstacle to expanding their businesses, according to women in La Paz, El Alto, Cochabamba, and Santa Cruz, is the lack of operating capital. All participants working in six different sectors shared this view, but women running small grocery stores and food vendors strongly supported this view. Women working in camelid and textiles also strongly lamented the lack of physical capital, especially machinery.

Given the strength of the micro-finance sector in Bolivia and the range of organizations that provide poor people, in particular women, with direct access to credit, small loans would seem an obvious solution to cash- and equipment-strapped female business owners. But the women participants in the focus group discussions did not concur.

On the contrary, the women greatly mistrusted credit institutions and feared the consequences of taking on debt. These negative perceptions applied both to formal banks and micro-finance institutions and were based on both their own and peers' experiences. The heavy burden of repayment was a common theme for some (*"I've had to work three times as hard in order to pay the bank,"*) while others told personal stories of default and loss of assets. Women agreed that interest rates are set prohibitively high and that *"in the end, you end of working only to pay off loans."* Some women were even more pessimistic: *"I have seen what they've done to friends of mine … I prefer not to get loans because in the end you lose everything you have."*

In most groups, a few women still viewed credit as a potential way to expand their businesses. But these women noted that even if one wanted credit, it wasn't always easy to get. They cited obstacles in obtaining credit, such as the lack of legal documents and collateral. Said one woman: *"The banks demand a lot in terms of papers and guarantees. They ask for papers and titles of the house, documents related to income, guarantors, they ask how many kids you have and a bunch of other questions."*

Finally, with the exception of single women who noted that banks often asked for a husband to co-sign loans, the women did not feel that they were treated differently from men when applying for credit. Any differences there are, the women explained, are due to other differences: *"They lend less money to women but that's because we have lower incomes."*

*Source: Informe Estudio Cualitativo: Informalidad y Productividad*, Encuestas y Estudios (2007).

Although women's aversion to credit is partly attributable to their perception of punitively high interest rates, interest rates are in fact reasonable by regional standards. Naturally, credit is more costly the more informal the provider, and women rely more heavily on informal sources of credit. Comparing formal bank loans and micro-credit loans—and considering that it is costlier and riskier to lend to a small, informal firm than to a larger firm—the difference in interest rates between the two is actually relatively small in Bolivia (World Bank 2007). Furthermore, in comparing the rates charged by different micro-finance institutions in the region, Bolivian institutions seem to operate with some of the lowest interest rates (Appendix 4).

Lack of land and property titles, which are often required as collateral, may also discourage female demand for credit. The focus groups debated how the lack of documents establishing ownership of their land or house makes it difficult to establish collateral. Although land-titling practices in Bolivia are currently changing, with many more joint titles (58 percent), titles exclusively for women are still rare (6 percent) relative to titles awarded to men (24 percent).[2] Looking at a sample of Latin American countries, Deere and Leon (2003) find that roughly 70–90 percent of formal owners of farmland are men, and that when women do own farmland, their holdings are typically smaller than men's.[3]

In terms of supply-side constraints, the qualitative data reveal no evidence of gender-based discrimination in access to credit. Few have claimed that financial institutions discriminate against women, and female firm owners typically state that banks simply *"lend less money to women because we have lower incomes."* As noted earlier, Bolivia's vibrant micro-finance industry is dominated by women and there is little discrimination against women in this sector. The few women who cited unfair and prejudiced practices by banks were either single or divorced; they claimed banks excluded them by requiring a husband's signature or guarantee.

According to focus groups, the strongest supply-side constraint is the "inappropriateness" of financial services offered to women. Several focus groups noted that the financial instruments offered by banks or micro-finance institutions are either insufficiently flexible to allow women to respond to changing opportunities or are unsuitable for their specific needs. This concern was particularly strong in focus groups with women from certain sectors. For example, women who run grocery stores or sell food concerned with managing day-to-day cash shortfalls are best served by financial services akin to working capital credit lines. Women in other sectors cited the need to invest in new machinery (camelid and textiles) and thus the need for regular investment credit. In these sectors, concerns centered on the perceived high interest rates.

Estimates suggest that removing constraints to capital for female–owned firms can be highly profitable, depending on the sector. Estimates of the internal rate of return of doubling the capital of firms in each of the six sectors by gender show that in food sales, textiles, and camelid, returns are high for women, and indeed higher than for men (Table 3.2). In contrast, further investment in grocery stores does not appear attractive for female firm owners. While these are rough estimates, they indicate the need for a sector-specific approach to interventions aimed at expanding female enterprises. The results also reflect the current under-investment in women's businesses relative to men's in both camelid and textiles. As noted earlier, these are also the two sectors where men operate productive asset levels that are four-six times as large as women.

**Table 3.2. Internal Rates of Return for a Doubling of Capital, by Sector and Gender**

|  | Textiles | Transportation | Grocery stores | Food sales | Wood products | Camelid products |
|---|---|---|---|---|---|---|
| Men | 9 | −10 | 4 | 32 | 2 | 4 |
| Women | 27 | −13 | −7 | 37 | 4 | 18 |

*Source:* Authors' estimation based on information in the 2007 micro and small enterprise survey.
*Note:* There are only six observations of male owners in the camelid sector, three observations of female owners in transportation, and nine observations of female owners in wood products.

Women's desire to expand their businesses also varies depending on the sector, but it tends to be less strong than men's. The micro-enterprise survey results indicate that women who run grocery stores have no wish to expand current operations, while men in this sector do. On the other hand, women in textiles expressed a strong wish to expand, estimating the ideal size of their operation at 13 employees, compared with the current average of 2. Rough estimates show that doubling the capital of women in this sector would boost monthly profits by about 22 percent, which implies an internal rate of return on the required investment of about 27 percent.

*Access to Physical, Social, and Human Capital*

Women's concerns regarding access to physical capital vary by sector, with women in some sectors focusing on machinery and others on the need for larger inventories. Focus groups in the textile and camelid sectors signaled a particular need for more machinery and equipment. Women operate with significantly fewer assets than men in both sectors, while rough estimates show especially high internal rates of return on further investments in female-owned enterprises. Focus groups with women running grocery stores, or engaged in food sales, focused on their inability to build and maintain adequate stocks of supplies.

Women operate with lower levels of physical assets because of their lower reliance on financial services, their different motivations for being in business, and their tendency to operate home-based businesses. Female-owned businesses are less likely to rely on financial services, which limit their ability to expand and invest in physical assets. Furthermore, if a woman's motivation for her business is solely to complement her husband's income when needed, a low level of investment in machinery and inventory makes sense because it allows for operations to adjust more easily to changes in husband's employment status. In addition, many female-owned businesses are run out of the home, which limits any major expansion. Finally, as women typically work from home, physical capital becomes fungible between the family and the business.

Trust or social capital among women is low in terms of their attitudes toward associating or partnering with other women. One way to share the costs of investing in new machinery, realize economies of scale in operations, and expand business would be to partner with other small-scale firm owners. Women did not, however, see this as a viable strategy for expansion. Female owners were forceful in stating that they would rather operate at a small scale and in a family-based structure than associate with other women. The lack of trust is shared by focus groups in all sectors (Box 3.3).

Female firm owners are more likely to join associations but many women think these are of no use. Women are more likely to join an association, even if it promises no clear benefit (Figure 3.3). Forty five percent of women and 32 percent of men feel that participating in an association offers no benefits (Figure 3.4). The most important reason for women to associate is to protect a location (noted by 16 percent of women), while men associate in order to access financing (15 percent) and to negotiate with the government (13 percent).

**Box 3.3. Female Firm Owners' Perceptions of the Benefits of Organizing**

Many women lack faith in the utility of associations. Female entrepreneurs in focus group discussions in La Paz, El Alto, Cochabamba, and Santa Cruz felt that a highly individualistic stance would most benefit their businesses. The women typically rejected the option of setting up or joining associations and cooperatives, for three reasons: First, they had little trust in the honesty of others and in working together with others for a common good. Second, they tended to equate membership in associations with a loss of independence and a potential loss of control over their own resources. Third, they viewed associations largely as not helpful in expanding businesses.

Some women agreed that working with others to address issues like market access, safety, or training might help, but none were willing to share productive resources or assets if it limited their scope for expanding their business. The three reasons cited above were debated by a few women in each group, who cited such areas as training where joining with other women did not threaten their business and might make sense. But all agreed that common ownership or sharing of assets of any kind was completely out of the question. One woman summed up the general view this way: "*It's better to keep it small but in your own hands.*"

*Source: Informe Estudio Cualitativo: Informalidad y Productividad*, Encuestas y Estudios (2007).

**Figure 3.3. Firms' Membership in Associations, by Gender (% of Firms)**

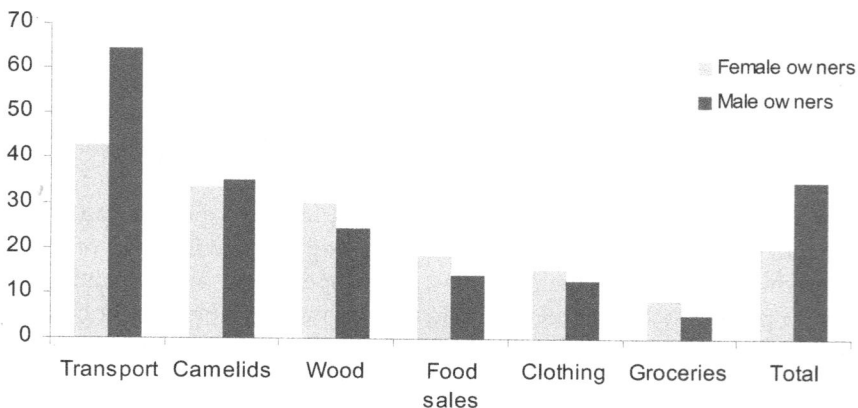

*Source*: Authors' calculations based on World Bank Micro Enterprises Survey, 2007.
*Note*: There are only six observations of male owners in the camelid sector, three observations of female owners in transportation, and nine observations of female owners in wood products.

**Figure 3.4. Benefits of Associations, by Gender (% of Firms)**

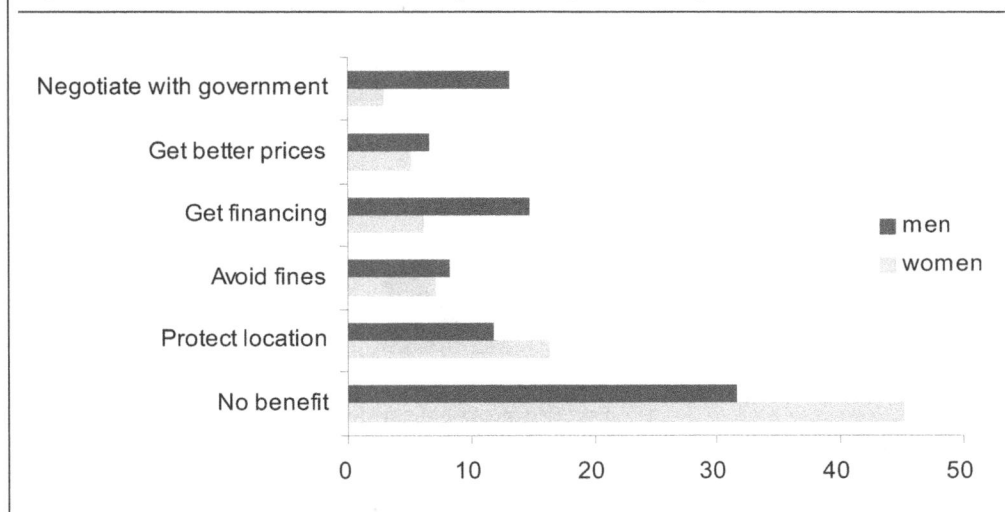

*Source*: Authors' calculations based on World Bank Micro Enterprises Survey, 2007.

In terms of human capital, female firm owners face severe constraints to productivity owing to their lower educational levels, a constraint that is particularly binding for indigenous women. The fact that women, particularly indigenous women, have significantly lower levels of schooling relative to their male peers undermines their ability to adopt the best procedures for expanding their firms, such as applying for loans or formalizing their businesses. Indigenous women in El Alto also cited difficulties in accessing and making sense of information needed to export.

Owing to women's lower education, access to skilled labor may also constrain female-owned enterprises because women prefer to hire women and the sectors they work in tend to be populated by women. While lower education levels of female business owners limit productivity, their propensity to hire other women results in a workforce that also has lower levels of education and productivity. Needless to say, women in sectors strongly dominated by women tend not to hire men. But apart from the obvious reasons for this are others that are more cultural in nature. Some women felt that men might not be comfortable working for women; others said that their husbands would not look favorably upon them hiring men. Interestingly, the propensity of women to hire women seems to fall with firm size (Figure 3.5). Again, we account for sectoral influences on hiring patterns.

## Market and Home-Based Constraints to Women's Economic Productivity

In some sectors, women face barriers to accessing new markets; in others the main concern is strong price competition. The female business owners participating in our focus groups frequently cited as constraints to expanding their businesses markets that are too small and harsh competition, which result in low profit margins.

**Figure 3.5. Female Employees as Share of Total, by Firm Size and Gender of Owner**

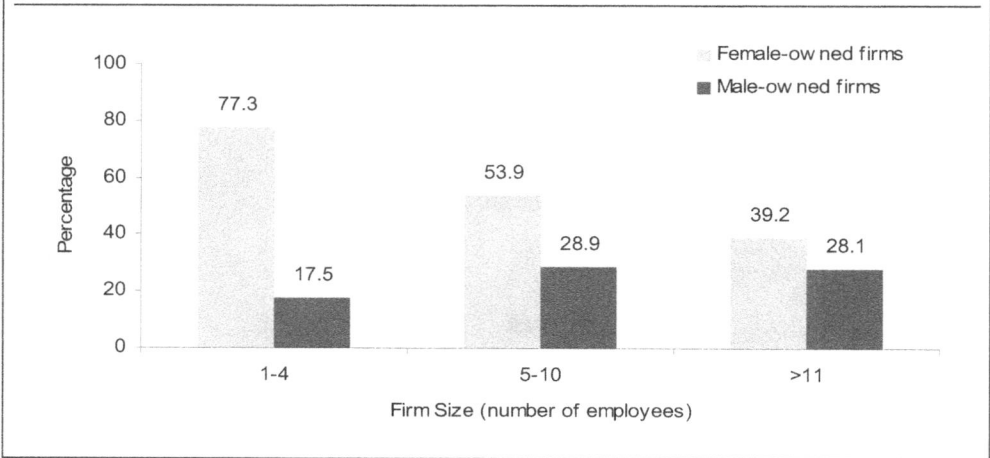

*Source*: Authors' calculations based on World Bank Micro Enterprises Survey, 2007.
*Note*: There are only six observations of male owners in the camelid sector.

Many also noted how these factors led to insecure and highly variable income streams. Concerns about market access and competition seem to be sector-specific and to apply to both men and women. Women engaged in selling food or running grocery stores emphasized the importance of competitive pressure. In textiles, the key concern was imports of used clothes, which are putting downward pressures on prices.[4] Female firm owners working in the camelid sector argued that the lack of information and support from the government was blocking their access to export markets. The aspirations to export were strong in this sector and seemed fuelled by stories of Peruvian successes in exporting alpaca and alpaca-derived products.

In some sectors, women viewed extortion and harassment by enforcement agents as limiting their productivity and hampering their incentives to formalize their businesses. Women selling prepared food in particular felt that the competitive pressures on the streets increased the scope for public officials to extort 'contributions' from vendors seeking to keep their spot in a market or on a street. Camelid producers who sell their products on the street alluded to similar problems. The women felt that by formalizing their businesses, the problem of corruption and extortions would only become worse as it would put them under greater scrutiny. Typical comments expressed during focus groups include: *"The police always extort us and put pressure on us for the smallest things. If we register this will surely get worse,"* and *"The municipality intimidates us, if we formalize, worse things will follow."*

Domestic responsibilities shape women's motivations for entering business and can stifle female business owners' aspirations and their ability to expand. As noted in Chapter 2, women's preference for self-employment reflects their need to accommodate childcare, household chores, and their husbands' employment. And women who choose to work from home for its added flexibility to care for their families and homes may not be looking to expand their businesses; this, in turn, limits the productivity gains associated with increasing scale.

With the exception of textiles, women work no fewer hours than men (Figure 3.6). When women refer to "double" workloads attributable to their need to balance home and work responsibilities, they mean just that. Their need for flexible hours and autonomy in the workplace is high and creates barriers against moving into formal employment or into more productive sectors. It may also deter aspirations to expand the scale of their operations. The qualitative data do not explain the gender difference in work hours in textiles.

---

**Box 3.4. Why Female Firm Owners Prefer Informality**

Women see informality as a way to balance productive and reproductive roles, and to complement household income. While the issue of balancing family and domestic responsibility did not emerge in focus group discussions organized with predominantly men, it was a central theme among the women participating in female focus groups. Says one woman: "*A woman has to work triple: the home, the children and in addition, the business. This particular line of work allows me to take care of my home and my children and I don't have to leave my house.*" The other main reason for self-employment that emerged from the qualitative data was the need to complement household income.

Some women also noted that they entered self-employment in response to mobility constraints imposed by husbands. In other words, women's mobility is sometimes constrained by gender roles, as exemplified by statements such as: "*My husband won't let me work outside our home.*" Similarly, some women invoked jealousy and *machismo* as important obstacles to looking for jobs outside the home.

*Source: Informe Estudio Cualitativo: Informalidad y Productividad*, Encuestas y Estudios (2007).

---

**Figure 3.6. Hours Worked per Week, by Gender and Sector**

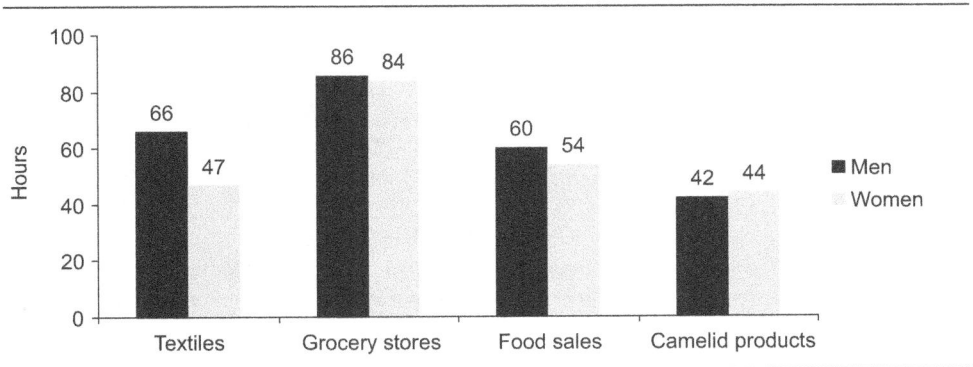

*Source*: Authors' calculations based on World Bank Micro Enterprises Survey, 2007.
*Note*: There are only six observations of male owners in the camelid sector.

Evidence show that when child care constraints are loosened, women's labor force participation and economic activity rises. Empirical evidence from Colombia (Peña-Parga and Glassman 2004; Ribero 2003) and from Chile (Acosta, Perticara, and Ramos 2005) shows a strong relationship between access to child care and female labor force participation. At the same time, evidence from Mexico (Wong and Levine 1992, Gong and van Soest 2002) shows that labor market participation of women with young children increases when they live in households with other adult women who can replace them as childcare providers during work hours. Chapter 4 will address the remarkable and rapid increase in women's economic activity resulting from expanded childcare services for low-income households in Guatemala and Mexico.

The prevalence of domestic violence is high in Bolivia and affects the autonomy and productive capacities of women.[5] The findings of a recent survey of domestic violence carried out by the Ministry of Health and Sports and the Pan American Health Organization (PAHO) show that 55.4 percent, 5 in every 10 respondents, had been victims of intra-family violence (*Programa Nacional Genero y Violencia* 2004). A cursory glance at estimates from other countries suggests that the prevalence of gender-based violence in Bolivia is high by regional standards (ECLAC 2007b).[6] Intimate partner violence was raised by some focus group participants, typically street food vendors, as a constraint in their business activity. Since these women depend on a loyal client base, offering a friendly service is key to good business.[7] According to the women, doing so without triggering their husbands' jealousy can be a difficult balancing act. Focus group discussions also revealed that some women are not allowed to work outside the home. Estimates from Latin America show that gender-based violence reduces not women's productivity and income (Morrison and Orlando 1999, 2004).Restrictions on women's autonomy imposed by spouses, for instance, in terms of mobility and "conduct," further reduces women's productive capabilities.

## Notes

[1] The consulting firm Encuestas y Estudios conducted the focus group interviews in June 2007. The firm directly extended invitations to a sample of firms that met the specifications required. See Encuestas y Estudios (2007). More on the selection process of sectors can be found in World Bank (2007).

[2] World Bank (2005).

[3] The sample includes Brazil, Chile, Colombia, Ecuador, Honduras, Mexico, Paraguay, and Peru.

[4] A study by the Bolivian Institute of International Commerce (IBCE) suggests that the importation of used clothes costs Bolivia about 15,300 jobs annually, and that 93 percent of imports are illegal (Vidaurre 2005).

[5] The prevalence of domestic violence is high in Bolivia, also by regional standards, and further work is needed to assess the impact of this on women's autonomy and productive capacities

[6] Estimates of gender-based violence are often not comparable in strict methodological terms, as they are derived from different survey instruments.

[7] The food sector is heterogeneous and includes women who bring cheap lunches to their clients' workplace (typically construction workers, police men, and other street vendors) or street vendors with specialized food stalls as well as owners of full-fledged restaurants. Building a loyal client base is key to all these businesses.

# CHAPTER 4

# Implications of Policies to Increase the Formalization and Productivity of Female Owners of Small and Micro Firms

In this chapter, we discuss policy options aimed at promoting increased growth and productivity of female-owned small and micro firms in Bolivia, rather than promoting formalization as an end in itself. This is because, as noted earlier, most female-owned informal businesses in Bolivia are simply too small to benefit from becoming formal, and the disadvantages (e.g., tax and registration payments and bureaucratic requirements) are too great for a struggling small business. Therefore, policies that make it easier and more profitable for women to expand their businesses, and thus reap the economic benefits of formalization, are likely to be most successful. However, policymakers should also sustain and accelerate additional measures related to administrative simplification and information flow with respect to formalization in parallel with the policy options we propose below.[1]

Women's businesses are on average too small to benefit from formalization and policies should focus on relieving constraints to productivity and growth. Given the concentration of women in this segment, micro firms are the main focus of this chapter. The policy options we identify are aimed at either increasing access to productive input factors (such as finance, human capital, technology, raw materials, and machinery) or reducing constraints on women's productive participation in economic activities in the market (such as barriers to entering markets, mobility constraints attributable to crime, or corruption and abuse by public officials) and at home (such as double workloads caused by household chores and childcare, gender-based violence, and other constraints to women's autonomy).

Some of the policies to boost productivity and growth can be combined with measures to expand the benefits of formalization, as an added incentive for women business owners to formalize. The benefits of formalization could be increased in a wide variety of ways, including by making business development and training services available to formal firms; widening their public procurement opportunities; developing domestic markets with products of better quality and price; improving formal export promotion programs; and by supporting supplier development programs aimed at increasing linkages with larger private firms. Other ways of making formality more attractive include linking formalization with access to credit and improving the quality of legal services available to small businesses. In order to reach women, interventions to enhance the benefits of formality need to be made relevant for the sectors in which women operate. But priority should be given to facilitating productivity and business growth; the authorities need to be careful not to exclude the informal sector from training, business linkage, and credit access programs.

Policies to facilitate the growth and increased productivity of female-owned businesses have two main objectives: promoting gender equality in access to productive assets; and creating an enabling environment for female entrepreneurship.

Three priority areas of intervention to promote women's access to productive assets are:

- Short term: Expand and enhance women's use of **credit and financial services** by focusing on demand-side constraints (aversion to obtaining credit, lack of information and the skills needed to complete the loan application process, lack of trust in the benefits of associating with other women, and group guarantees for loans) and supply-side constraints (such as collateral and other loan requirements, identity documents, co-signatures, and earnings statements). Gender differences in access to formal land and property titles—and the use of these as collateral—also needs to be assessed.

- Short to medium term: Provide **training** to women targeted to their areas of economic activity to build entrepreneurial ability and self-confidence (self-efficacy).

- Medium to long-term: Address gender inequities in **formal education,** focusing especially on indigenous women. As women tend to hire women, closing gender gaps in human capital endowments also raises the productivity of workers in female-run firms.

Three priority areas of interventions to expand women's choices and create an enabling environment for them to respond to market opportunities are:

- Short to medium term: Ease home-related constraints, in particular those posed by **childcare,** by facilitating expanded coverage of day-care services and/or adapting existing services to the needs of working mothers.

- Medium term: Help female-owned businesses **access new markets** (e.g., niche markets and export markets) and **increase competitiveness in existing markets**.

- Long term: Address root causes of gender-based occupational segregation to make the choice of entering low-productivity sectors and occupations a matter of 'true' preference.

Policies cannot take one-size-fits-all approaches. Productivity constraints to female entrepreneurship take numerous forms, and affect women differently depending on individual and business characteristics. Growth constraints and requirements differ according to sector, indicating a need for sector-specific assessments and solutions (which is outside the scope of this report). Women's needs in terms of access to financial and physical assets and markets vary across sectors and by enterprise characteristics, especially scale of operations. Human capital constraints—in formal schooling and business skills—are more generalized issues in Bolivia, but special policies are needed here as well to address the multiple constraints facing indigenous women. Finally, the importance of home-based constraints depends critically on family/marital status and household composition (number of young children and elderly), and any interventions need to be designed with these variables in mind.

## Promoting Women's Access to Productive Assets

The following policy options are targeted at closing gaps in the endowment of productive assets of male and female firm owners. Policies are divided into two areas: increasing access by women to credit and other financial services, and promoting greater human and social capital accumulation by women. In practice, some of these policy options could be combined, for example, by programs linking greater access to bank credit with business training.

*Credit and Other Financial Services*

Better access to financial services has the potential to raise the productivity of some female-owned firms. Access to finance allows for better inputs, increased working capital, funding new investment, equipment maintenance, and training for employers. However, female firm owners constitute a heterogeneous group with different aspirations and abilities, and international evidence suggests that the returns to capital vary widely among women. A recent experiment with micro enterprises in Sri Lanka shows that while monthly average returns for female owners was zero or negative, more than 40 percent of women still earned mean returns of 5 percent or more (Box 4.1).

Fostering higher demand for credit among women can be accomplished more effectively through simple marketing tactics than through lowered interest rates. The qualitative data showed how focus groups of women viewed interest rates as punitively high and as a possible deterrent to applying for loans. In South Africa, a consumer finance lender evaluated the sensitivity to interest rates (Karlan and Zinman 2006c; Karlan and Zinman 2006a), as well as the effectiveness of different marketing approaches, on the likelihood that individuals borrowed. The authors find that some costless marketing approaches—such as presenting only one rather than several loans or including a woman's photo on the mailer—were as effective in increasing demand as reducing the interest rate as much as 4 percentage points a month from an average rate of 8 percent across the sample (Bertrand, Karlan, Mullainathan, and others 2005).

---

**Box 4.1. Gender-Based Differences in the Returns to Capital**

---

A recent experiment amongst Sri Lankan micro enterprises found dramatically different returns by gender. While the average male firm owner enjoys returns in excess of 9 percent a month, the average returns for female owners are zero or even negative. This, of course, is insufficient to cover the relatively high costs of micro loans. As noted by the authors of the study, this indicates that permanently raising the income of women that run micro enterprises may be more difficult than raising the income of men in similar conditions.

Gender-based sectoral segregation seems to be the key explanation for the lack of returns among female owners. Low returns were not the result of women taking the grants out of the business and spending them on household investments, nor the result of differences in the ability of male and female owners. The study suggests that part of the effect is because women concentrate in different industries than men. Yet, even when women work in the same industries as men, their returns tend to be lower.

However, the zero average return does not imply that no female-owned enterprises earn high returns. Forty percent of female-owned firms earned a mean return of 5 percent or more. Thus, there is still a subset of female-owned firms that generates sufficient returns to cover the cost of loans.

*Source*: De Mel, McKenzie, and Woodruff (2007).

---

Access to credit is affected by gender inequalities in the distribution of property rights and other practical obstacles, such as lacking identification, and in the case of indigenous women, language, and cultural barriers. Most formal property titles throughout Latin America are held by men, and those held by women tend to be smaller than men's. This limits the ability of women to use property titles as collateral to access credit. The government has recently introduced additional measures to enforce gender equality in land regularization. For example, rural property ownership titles resulting from registration and land distribution must now include the names of both the head of the household and the spouse, and the women's name is listed first. However, unless the women and the front personnel of micro-finance institutions understand how joint titles are used as collateral for loans, simply adding the woman's name to a title will not increase women's access to credit. The need for information is particularly grave among indigenous women who have less education. Some women—again, predominantly indigenous women—even lack valid national identity cards. Finally, impact evaluations of land titling programs in the region suggest that property titles are necessary but not always sufficient to access credit (Box 4.2).

The positive effects of a credit expansion may remain limited unless women's access to complementary resources is improved and additional constraints addressed. Easing the constraints attributable to market imperfections, low human and social capital, and the heavy burden of household chores would help facilitate resource mobility and thus enhance the effectiveness of credit expansion.

---

**Box 4.2. Property and Land Titles: Necessary but not Sufficient to Access Credit?**

---

Latin America has seen a series of land titling programs in the past decades, many with a primary objective of promoting access to credit. With formal titles in hand, it was expected that families would gain access to bank credit using their property as collateral. Yet, available impact evaluations have shown mixed results. In Argentina, evaluations found that even after households gained land titles, other requirements for obtaining loans—such as formal employment status and personal documentation—still blocked their access to credit (Galiani and Schargrodsky, 2005). In Peru, the land titling project did reduce the share of households defined as lacking collateral, but this, it turned out, was not the primary credit constraint on households. Instead, risk exposure determined access to credit, and the ability to manage risk was not affected (Boucher and others 2007). Finally, in Uruguay, Gandelman (2007) shows that property ownership does not increase access to loans in formal or informal financial institutions. The main requirements were a personal identity document and some form of documentation of their wages, while only 4 percent of loan applicants were asked to present a property title.

*Source: Outsiders? The Changing Patterns of Exclusion in Latin America and the Caribbean* (IADB 2007).

---

*Building Human and Social Capital*

Policies to build human and social capital include: addressing gaps in formal education, bundling credit and other financial services with training, and promoting associative activity to build self-efficacy in women business owners and to give voice to women's concerns. Interventions to raise the formal education of women—in particular indigenous women—are urgently needed, and returns are high, especially in the long term. Providing training in business skills, together with credit, has been shown to produce quick wins for both lenders and borrowers. Fostering women's associative activity could also produce important results in the short to medium term, but the government's role, beyond creating an enabling environment, is unclear.

Gaps in formal education tend to segregate women into low-productivity sectors and occupations, and limit the profitability of female-owned firms and female owners' self-efficacy. Literature on the impact of education irrefutably shows that better educational outcomes for women lead to higher labor force participation and earnings, and better prepares women for the challenges of running their own business.[2] There are also important ethnic dimensions to the distribution of years of schooling throughout the population, with indigenous women receiving less education than any other group. As such, policies should address not only male/female gaps, but also the indigenous/non-indigenous gap with an aim to improve the in some cases abysmal lags still experienced by indigenous women. Policies regarding formal education are not discussed in detail here. However, earlier assessments of the educational challenges facing Bolivia cite the need for both supply-side interventions—especially in rural and indigenous areas—as well as demand-side interventions such as conditional cash transfers (World Bank 2006). The latter has proved effective in raising girls' enrollment (Schultz 2004, Skoufias and Parker 2001) as well as for indigenous children (Bando and others 2005). The Morales administration's introduction of a cash transfer for grades 1-5 in primary school (called *Juancito Pinto*) is a first step to closing gender and ethnic gaps in education. There may be a rationale for extending this program to secondary students, in order to increase attendance and educational outcomes of children, especially indigenous girls. While this may help level educational outcomes, the quality of the education offered is another pressing issue and a potential source of inequities.

Well-designed training programs can build self-efficacy among female firm owners and increase the impact of credit. Policy could be aimed at building the self-efficacy of owners of small and micro firms through training, including using successful entrepreneurs to share ideas and mentor others. As noted in World Bank (2007), increasing the self-efficacy of business owners may affect their motivation to expand a business. Training can also help increase the impact of credit by focusing on building financial literacy and other business skills of borrowers to put credit to more effective use. This argues for bundled delivery of financial services and capacity building. Offering training alongside small loans enhances economic outcomes for both female borrowers and lending institutions. The *Servicio Nacional de Desarrollo Productivo del Pequeño Productor* (SENADEPRO) and subsidized loans from government is currently developing a bundle of services by offering training and capacity building alongside the Banco de Desarollo Productivo (BDP). However, these programs do not target women specifically. The FINCA program in Peru (Box 4.3) provides an example of bundled services targeted at women. The Peru program was aimed at improving basic business practices (such as how to treat clients) and improving the goods and services produced. It also taught women how to use profits, where to sell, and how to use special discounts and credit sales.

Strengthening women's formal or informal systems of organizing, networking, and information sharing is another way to bridge the capability gap between men and women and promote self-efficacy. Although the potential benefits of training seem obvious, many poor women, especially very small producers and market vendors, are unable to put their acquired skills into practice. Some researchers have suggested that systems of networking and information exchange may often be more valuable interventions than skills and business training alone (Mayoux 1995).

---

**Box 4.3. The Role of Training in Raising the Self-Efficacy of Self-Employed Women in Peru**

---

Karlan and Valdivia (2006) measure the marginal impact of teaching basic business skills to self-employed Peruvian women enrolled in the group lending program FINCA. They do so by conducting a randomized control trial in which preexisting credit groups are randomly assigned to either credit with education (business training only) or to credit only (i.e., no change to their services). Their evaluation finds that training improves business knowledge, practices, and revenue for female entrepreneurs, and also leads to higher repayment and client retention rates for the lending institution. In short, providing entrepreneurial training alongside credit improves the economic outcomes for both women entrepreneurs and micro-credit institutions.

*Source*: Kaplan and Valdivia (2006), World Bank (2007).

Carr and Chen (2004) note that while workers in the informal economy were until recently considered unorganized by definition, recent evidence suggests that the informal workforce is being organized by formal trade unions, alternative trade unions, and pro-labor NGOs. Examples are the Self-Employed Women's Association in India (Box 4.4) and the international alliance of street vendors, StreetNet. Cooperatives are another form through which self-employed women organize and build systems of mutual support and information exchange. Bolivian examples exist, such as the Domestic Workers' Union. The role of such networks in building capabilities in female firm owners needs to be carefully assessed and supported when appropriate.

Interventions need to take into account local and national preferences and tastes for associative activity. Both focus group discussions and the firm survey reveal a lack of trust among Bolivian women in the benefits of organizing. While working with others to address such issues as market access, safety, or training could be an alternative for some, none were willing to share productive resources or assets if it meant foregoing opportunities to expand their business. At the same time, the government's role in fomenting such associations is not clear, and its effectiveness in doing so is unclear. A first step would be to create public spaces in which self-employed women can meet to exchange ideas and learn from each others' experiences, if possible, by teaming up with local or international NGOs.

---

**Box 4.4. The Role of Business Associations in Raising the Self-Efficacy of Self-Employed Women**

---

The Self-Employed Women's Association (SEWA) in India is a prime example of the successful organization of self-employed women. Founded by a trade union organizer in 1972 as a union of women workers in the informal economy, SEWA had to spend over 2 years to be registered as a trade union, over 10 years to be recognized by some of the International Trade Secretariats, over 20 years to be invited to join the National Labor Congress of India, and 30 years to be invited to be an official member of the worker delegation from India to the International Labor Conference. In trying to gain official recognition within the international labor movement, SEWA has served as a worldwide inspiration for the women's movement, the micro-finance movement, and a growing movement of informal workers and producers.

In Durban, South Africa, the Self-Employed Women's Union (SEWU) has actively forced progressive and gender-sensitive measures on the city's policies toward the informal economy. SEWU focuses on empowering its members, and frequent workshops are designed to build necessary skills, such as chairing meetings, negotiating, resolving conflicts, running organizations, and understanding local government operations. Other smaller towns in South Africa have established user-friendly systems for resolving conflicts that arise between the local authorities and informal traders in which a trader who feels wronged by any municipal decision can go to an appeals committee of five members, of whom at least one has to be a street trader.

*Sources:* Carr and Chen (2004), Lund and Skinner (2003), Skinner (2006).

## Providing an Enabling Environment for Women's Entrepreneurship

To expand women's choices and create an enabling environment for women to respond to market opportunities, three priority interventions include easing home-related constraints, in particular those posed by childcare; helping female-owned businesses access new markets (e.g., niche markets and export markets); and addressing the root causes of gender-based occupational segregation.

### Addressing Constraints in Market Access and Competitiveness

Associating with other women can help women strengthen their call for the government to address crime and corruption and help create a safe working environment, including freedom from harassment. Self-employed women (e.g., camelid traders and street food vendors) reported incidents of abuse and extortion by municipal authorities and public officials; as a result, women's trust in local government is low. Food vendors also complained about the lack of cleanliness in the public spaces where they trade. Strengthening associations of traders and street food vendors can be an effective way of improving abusive work environments (Levine and others 1999, Tokman 2001). Such associations can help informal firms as well as public health and safety by: giving stronger political voice to the concerns of small-scale entrepreneurs and facilitating a more effective engagement with local authorities, and developing self-regulatory mechanisms for informal trade activities. SEWA in India and SEWU in South Africa are examples of the power of such initiatives (Box 4.4). As noted above, the role of government policy in this area is limited mainly to helping increase information flow on the benefits of association.

The Bolivian government should explore sector-specific approaches that address problems of market access and competitiveness, with a view to facilitating women's entry into niche and/or export markets. A key constraint that emerged from focus group discussions was stiff competition and consequent low profit margins, coupled with restricted access to niche and export markets. Women perceived their markets as too small and too competitive. An important policy objective to promote the growth and productivity of small businesses, in general, and female-owned firms in particular, is providing adequate support systems with useful information, technical assistance, advice and guidance. Such support systems can be tailored to sectors looking to export (camelid) on the one hand, or/and sectors where moving into niche markets may make more sense (textile manufacturing and food sales), on the other. India's government has created a supportive environment for exporting in the artisan and crafts sector by making research, technology, and funding readily available to artisans (Box 4.5). Linking these programs to ones facilitating formalization (e.g., offering more extensive training, services, and market opportunities to firms that become formal) could further strengthen their impact.[3] The government, through the Vice Ministry of Micro and Small Firms, is considering expanding the benefits to formal firms in order to provide incentives for formalization. The programs envisaged need to take into account how the incentives to formalize depend crucially on firm size. They may also want to include benefits that cater in particular to the needs of sectors in which female-run businesses concentrate.

---

**Box 4.5. Policy Support to Artisans, India**

---

With a rich tradition of handicraft and artisan production, India has over the past 40 years designed specific policies to promote the sector. Most government assistance is for master artisans who sell both domestically and in international markets. Specific government measures have included: ministries for handicrafts; reservation of raw material and markets for designated products; research on designs and technologies; and various forms of funding and subsidies.

When India's economy liberalized, many artisans begun to access global markets, and the sector nearly doubled between 1991 and 1998. Recent estimates suggest the artisans contribute $5.6 billion to India's GDP and a significant part of the country's export earnings.

*Source*: WIEGO 2002, quoted in Chen and others 2004.

---

Non-governmental organizations, fair trade organizations, and private sector export initiatives can help create channels for women to access export and niche markets. NGOs and fair trade organizations provide alternative channels through which small-scale, often poor, producers can tap niche export markets. Fair trade organizations routinely focus on particularly disadvantaged groups such as women or indigenous peoples, and some estimate that between 70 and 80 percent of handicraft producers in fair trade are women (Redfern and Snedker 2002). Fair trade organizations and NGOs typically offer embedded services (e.g., training, market information, export facilitation) that these producers would not have been able to source locally or otherwise afford. Export channels, however, do not have to be non-profit in order to benefit poor women in the informal sector, as witnessed by the success of the web-based trading site BoliviaMall.com (Box 4.6).

---

**Box 4.6. Web-Based Handicrafts Exports From Bolivia**

---

BoliviaMall.com is the leader in e-business in Bolivia, exporting over 6,000 Bolivian products from 750 small vendors and artisans to more than 70 countries around the world. The company, which is entirely internet-based, has grown 5000 percent over the last six years. About 98 percent of the suppliers are informal. Most of the artisans are men, but often their wives manage the business, negotiate with the company, and handle the money. In March 2007, BoliviaMall took part in the "United Nations meets Silicon Valley" forum organized by Intel and the Global Alliance for ITC, to showcase how technology can help the poor.

*Source:* BoliviaMall press-release, March 9, 2007, as well as personal communication with Executive Director, Percy Prieto on 19 June 2007.

---

The development of business "clusters" is a second way to build capacity and facilitate entry into niche or export markets. A business cluster refers to a geographic concentration of interconnected businesses, suppliers, and associated institutions in a particular field. Clusters are considered to encourage competition and collaboration between businesses and can particularly benefit small firms as they enhance their ability to compete in global markets. Nadvi and Barrientos (2004) conclude that clusters can help create jobs and promote incomes for the poor, especially for marginalized segments of the labor force—such as women, migrants, and unskilled workers—first, by helping small and micro enterprises mobilize limited resources, and second, by providing necessary avenues for collective actions. An example from the textiles industry in Johannesburg highlights these and other issues (Box 4.7).

---

**Box 4.7. The Fashion District Initiative in Johannesburg**

The Johannesburg "Fashion District Initiative" is the city's strategy for integrating a cluster of informal garment enterprises into the formal economy based on the provision of storage and office space to informal firms in a specially designated "fashion district." The district covers 20 city blocks and the initiative involved some 1,000 clothing micro-manufacturers. The city also gave the firms training and advice on marketing and business development. Interventions took the form of a partnership between the city, provincial, and national governments; the private sector; and a tertiary training institution. Activities included training, the development of a training center, and the formation of a production network and an operators association.

Evaluations based on a controlled comparison found that the interventions led to higher levels of output and employment, as well as product diversification and competitive upgrading. The supported firms have developed a focus on niche markets, penetrating new markets both locally and even internationally. The output of firms involved in the initiative increased significantly, along with employment opportunities. Some estimates indicate that more than 1,000 jobs have been created. Networking between firms also increased, while outsourcing and integration of migrant workers has been encouraged.

*Source*: Kenyon 2007, Rogerson 2004.

---

Finally, rigid labor regulation that creates disincentives to hire women in the formal sector needs to be addressed. As discussed in Chapter 2, current labor laws dictate shorter work weeks for women, night work prohibition, weak domestic work regulations (e.g., irregular work hours) and employer-paid maternity benefits that cannot be shared by husbands. At the same time, provisions against discrimination in remuneration and merit promotion are weakly enforced. Together, these discourage formal employers from hiring women. Policymakers should thus consider eliminating sex-specific protective regulations and instead aim to protect workers through overtime limits that apply equally to both sexes. At the same time, the negative effect on female labor force participation from employer-financed maternity benefits can be mitigated through cost-sharing between employers, employees, and government, and by allowing that the maternity leave be shared with the husband (World Bank 2004).

*Address Gender-Specific Constraints at Home*

Publicly-supported childcare can free up time for women to expand their businesses or pursue better employment opportunities; it can also assure that women who choose self-employment do so voluntarily and not because they need to juggle their productive and reproductive roles. Evidence from Guatemala (Box 4.8) shows how access to childcare affects not only women's decision to work, but also the type of work they engage in and the amount of time they spend in paid work. The evidence from Mexico's new community-based program shows the potential for rapid results in terms of greater economic participation among beneficiary women. Only nine months into operations, nearly 80 percent of the women who initially did not work outside the house had entered the work force (Box 4.9).

Governments throughout Latin America are implementing a new generation of community-based childcare programs, in response to the need for more inclusive, lower cost childcare adapted to local needs. Throughout Latin America, childcare programs targeting working mothers with younger children (0–4 years of age) have sprung up in recent decades. Examples include the *Wawa Wasi* programs in Peru and Bolivia, *Hogares Comunitarios de Bienestar* in Colombia, and, most recently, the *Red the Instancias Infantiles* in Mexico (Box 4.9). The programs differ in size and scope, yet they share important design attributes, as they all: target low-income working mothers; focus on community involvement; rely on some form of co-responsibility scheme in which the state subsidizes the service and parents pay a fee depending on ability; and train caregivers in health, nutrition, and hygiene, as well as in psycho-pedagogical activities and early child development stimulation.

The current provision, and planned expansion, of childcare services should be assessed with regard to whether it responds to the needs of working women, especially those from low-income households. The government and international NGOs have operated with different types of community-based childcare in Bolivia (e.g., UNICEF's *Wawa Wasi* and the government's *Proyecto Integral de Desarrollo Infantil* program). Given these programs' focus on early child development, the impact on parents' economic activity, especially on working mothers, is not well documented.

---

**Box 4.8 Childcare in Guatemala City**

In poor urban neighborhoods of Guatemala City, finding affordable childcare is a challenge, especially since many poor mothers are migrants who live away from their extended family and have less access to informal alternative caregivers.

In Guatemala, the program *Hogares Comunitarios*, a government-sponsored day-care program, supports working parents and, in particular, mothers who are prime income earners. The program was set up to benefit two groups of women:

*Mothers of enrolled children.* These are mostly young working mothers, many single. They became more likely to be engaged in formal stable employment, possibly a result of having secured reliable and affordable childcare for extended hours. They also realize higher wages and a larger number of employment benefits than working mothers using alternative childcare arrangements.

*Caretakers are mothers themselves.* These are older, less educated women with more limited possibilities to work outside the home. They benefited through earning some (albeit low) income.

Although the childcare offered under the program was the cheapest alternative in the areas in which it operated, it was used by only 4 percent of eligible households. The evaluation states that this was due mainly to limited supply. The program was also found to improve food security and nutrition through cash transfers to caretaker mothers for food.

*Source:* Hallman et al 2003.

---

**Box 4.9. Red de Estancias Infantiles: A New Network of Day-Care Centers in Mexico**

---

In January 2007, Mexico established the *Red de Instancias Infantiles,* a network of day-care centers targeting at risk children ages 1–4 whose mothers or single fathers are currently working, looking to work, or studying. In the network's first year of operation, 97 percent of beneficiaries were women.

The co-responsibility **funding scheme** that the program has developed is based on subsidies for both providers and users, while households also pay providers a fee:

- Heads of households receive a subsidy of up to $64 per child, depending on household income.
- Heads of household then pay a fee to the provider of the day-care services. The fee varies with the subsidy received (larger the smaller the subsidy).
- Individuals or associations who wish to create a day-care center are provided a subsidy of up to $3,200 to prepare and equip the place in which they will provide childcare. Individuals or associations already in charge of day-care centers and who want to join the network receive a subsidy of up to $1,375 to help them ensure that their facility meets established standards.

In September 2007, 1,000 beneficiaries and nearly 300 day-care centers were surveyed. The results indicate potentially important **impacts** of the program in terms of facilitating the economic participation of women:

- When the day-care centers opened in January 2007, 29 percent of the beneficiaries did not work. Nine months later, 79 percent of those who were not working had entered the work force.
- By September 2007, one-fourth of the beneficiaries reported being in their first job, and, of these, 75 percent stated that the lack of childcare had previously prevented them from working.
- In total, 91 percent of beneficiaries work, 2 percent are studying, and the remainder is looking for jobs. Almost 15 percent were self-employed and over 70 percent were engaged in formal employment.

During 2007, the *Red de Estancias Infantiles* created 5,504 new day-care centers, and provided childcare to 115,100 children and 106,592 mothers. The program plans to open another 2,500 centers in 2008 in order to serve another 85,000 children. The assigned budget for 2008 is $132.6 million. The main challenges foreseen by the Ministry of Social Development (SEDESOL) during the extension of coverage are training of caregivers and quality control.

*Source:* www.sedesol.gob.mx. Presentation by SEDESOL during the World Bank virtual workshop *Childcare Policies and Gender Equality,* January 16. 2008.

---

There is little research, especially of a comparative nature, on the impact of different child-care strategies on women's economic activity. The differential impacts on working mothers' economic activity of program design or funding mechanisms is particularly poorly documented. Mexico's is an exception because of its clear focus on measuring the impact on working parents, while the child-care component of Chile's *Puente* program will be evaluated also in terms of its impact on female labor force participation. Households' demand for childcare services and, consequently, the impact on women's economic activity through increased labor force participation or entrepreneurial activity, depend on such design features as type of provider (community-based versus institutional), contribution schemes (publicly subsidized versus privately funded), and operational specifics (hours of operations and location). While regional lessons on program design remain elusive, European experience suggests that the more flexible the child care services, in particular in terms of hours, the easier it is for women to balance motherhood and work (Vegas and others 2006). Furthermore, strict quality control coupled with information campaigns on the beneficial effects of high-quality childcare on a child's development can help alleviate parents' concerns about leaving children in day care. Harder to combat are cultural attitudes that condemn women for working outside the home when children are young.

Policies that focus on prevention are essential for addressing the root causes of gender-based violence, another home-based productivity constraint. A recent review of interventions to combat gender-based violence (GBV) in Latin America concludes that prevention is best achieved by empowering women and reducing gender disparities, and by changing norms and attitudes that foster violence (Morrison and others 2004). Preventive policies range from community mobilization and mass media campaigns to change attitudes and behaviors, to school-based programs focused on changing male gender norms and training of law enforcement personnel about GBV-related legal reforms and the broader implications of GBV. To ensure the coherence of such multi-sectoral approaches, all interventions, be they preventive or targeted to assist victims (e.g., shelters and support groups), are best coordinated under a national plan. Latin America's experience shows that a justice system sensitized to GBV issues, and reinforced by new laws on women's rights, can act powerfully as agents of prevention, especially when enforcement of new laws is publicized (Morrison and others 2004).

### Addressing Gender-Based Occupational Segregation

The long-term goal of policies to address the concentration of women in low-productivity, informal employment is to make women's sector and occupational choice truly voluntary. While some occupational segregation reflects women's preferences for certain sectors and occupations, these alone cannot explain why the vast majority of Bolivian women concentrate in low-paying, low-productivity jobs. Interventions to foster female labor force participation—addressing gender gaps in education, providing health care, reforming labor laws that create disincentives for hiring women—are all key to reducing involuntary occupational segregation. Since occupational segregation is more pronounced among poorly educated women, policies need to target these women.

Additionally, more activist policies are needed to address gender stereotypes (Deutsch and others 2005). One set of interventions targets primary and secondary school students just when their choices begin to affect their future ability to enter certain occupations and ensures that non-sexist attitudes and gender roles are taught in textbooks and by teachers. A second set of interventions targets adult women (especially less educated women) with programs to facilitate their entry into non-traditional jobs. A prime example in Bolivia of such programs is PLANE (an employment program offering three-week public construction jobs on a lottery basis).

Although not initially targeted at women, recent estimates show that the vast majority of beneficiaries (85 percent) are women (Sierra and Calle 2006). In many cases, this program has given women their first-ever formal job with a salary. Women with experience from PLANE have since gone on to work in small municipal construction or maintenance projects. As a valuable side-effect, women also learn to set up day-care facilities for their children and solve other problems of working women (Sierra and Calle 2006).

## Notes

[1] The World Bank report "Policies for Increasing Firms' Formality and Productivity" (2007a) provides a detailed discussion of such measures.

[2] For a review of this literature, see Schultz (2002).

[3] *Policies for Increasing Firms' Formality and Productivity* (World Bank 2007a).

# References

Acosta, E., Perticara, M. y C. Ramos. 2007. Empleo Femenino: Oferta Laboral y Cuidado Infantil. BID.

Andersen, L. E. and B. Muriel. 2002. "Cantidad versus Calidad en Educación: Implicaciones para Pobreza" *Revista de Estudios Económicos y Sociales*, No. 1, pp. 11–41.

Ayyagari, Demirguc-Kunt and Maximovitch 2006. "The Role of finance in the business environment" World Bank Working Paper No 3820, Washington DC: World Bank.

Bando, R., L. F. Lopez-Calva, and H. A. Patrinos. 2005. "Child Labor, School Attendance, and Indigenous Households: Evidence from Mexico." Policy Research Working Paper 3487. World Bank, Washington, DC.

Bertrand, M., D. Karlan, S. Mullainathan, E. Shafir, and J. Zinman. 2005. "What's Psychology Worth? A Field Experiment in the Consumer Credit Market." Working Paper 918. Economic Growth Center, Yale University.

Boucher, S., B. Barham, and M. Carter. 2007. "Are Land Titles the Constraint to Enhance Agricultural Performance?" Unpublished.

Bravo, R., and D. Zapata. 2005. "Las metas del Milenio y la igualdad de género: El caso de Bolivia," Serie Mujer y Desarrollo 71. Santiago, Chile: CEPAL.

Buvinic, M. and J. Mazza. 2005. "Gender and Social Inclusion: Social Policy Perspectives from Latin America and the Caribbean," Conference Paper Arusha Conference, New Frontiers of Social Policy, December 12–15, 2005.

Carr, M., and M. Chen. 2004. "Globalization, Social Exclusion and Gender." *International Labor Review* 143(1–2).

De Mel, S., D. McKenzie, and C. Woodruff. 2007. "Measuring Microenterprise Profits: Don't Ask How the Sausage Is Made." Policy Research Working Paper Series 4229. World Bank, Washington, DC.

Deutsch, R., A. Morrison, C. Piras, and H. Nopo. 2005. "Working within Confines: Occupational Segregation by Gender in Three Latin American Countries." *The ICFAI Journal of Applied Economics* 0(3).

ECLAC. 2007a. "El aporte de las mujeres a la igualdad en América Latina y el Caribe," document prepared for the *X Conferencia Regional Sobre la Mujer de America Latina y Caribe*, Santiago, Chile: ECLAC.

———. 2007b. "¡Ni una mas! El derecho de vivir una vida libre de violencia en América Latina y el Caribe." Santiago, Chile: ECLAC.

Crenshaw, K. 2000. "The Intersectionality of Race and Gender Discrimination." Background paper presented at Expert Group Meeting on Gender and Race Discrimination, November 21–24, Zagreb, Croatia.

Cunningham, W. 2001. "Sectoral Allocation by Gender of Latin American Workers over the Liberalization Period of the 1990s." Policy Research Working Paper 2742. World Bank, Washington, DC.

Cunningham, W., and Carlos Ramos Gomez. 2004. "The Home as the Factory Floor: Employment and Remuneration of Home-based Workers," Policy Research Working Paper No. 3295. World Bank, Washington, DC.

Chen, M. 2001. "Women in the Informal Sector: A Global Picture the Global Movement." *SAIS Review* 21(1).

Chen, M., J. Vanek, M. Carr. 2004. *Mainstreaming Informal Employment and Gender in Poverty Reduction: A Handbook for Policy-makers and other Stakeholders.* The Commonwealth Secretariat, IDRC and WIEGO.

Deere, C., and M. Leon. 2003. "The Gender Asset Gap: Land in Latin America." *World Development* 31(6): 925–947.

Diagne, A., M. Zeller, and M. Sharma. 2000. "Empirical Measurements of Households' Access to Credit and Credit Constraints in Developing Countries: Methodological Issues and Evidence." IFPRI FCND Discussion Paper No. 90, Washington DC: International Food Policy Research Institute.

Doss, C. 2005. "The Effects of Intrahousehold Property Ownership on Expenditure Patterns in Ghana." *Journal of African Economies* 15.

Duflo, E. 2003. "Grandmothers and Granddaughters: Old Age Pension and Intra-Household Allocation in South Africa." *World Bank Economic Review* 17(1).

Duflo, E. and C.Udry. 2004. "Intrahousehold Resource Allocation in Côte d'Ivoire: Social Norms, Separate Accounts and Consumption Choices." NBER Working Paper No. 10498. National Bureau of Economic Research, Cambridge, MA.

Encuestas y Estudios. 2007. "Informe Estudio Cualitativo: Informalidad y Productividad, Grupos Focales Genero." La Paz, Bolivia: Encuestas y Estudios.

Galiani, S., and E. Schargrodsky. 2005. "Property Rights for the Poor: Effects of Land Titling." Universidad Torcuato Di Tella, Buenos Aires. Unpublished.

Gandelman, N. 2007. "The Impact of House Titling: Evidence from a Natural Experiment in Uruguay." PowerPoint presentation given at the Inter-American Development Bank seminar, Titling in Latin America: Effects and Channels, March 30, Washington, DC.

Gong, X., and A. van Soest. 2002. "Wage Differentials and Mobility in the Urban Labor Market: A Panel Data Analysis for Mexico." *Labor Economics* 9(4).

Hall, G., and H.A. Patrinos. 2006. *Indigenous Peoples, Poverty and Human Development in Latin America.* New York: Palgrave Macmillan.

Hallman, K., A.R. Quisumbing, M.T.Ruel and B. de la Briere. 2003. "Childcare and Work: Joint Decisions among Women in Poor Neighborhoods in Guatemala City." Washington DC: IFPRI.

Handa, S. 1996. "Expenditure Behavior and Children's Welfare: An Analysis of Female Headed Households in Jamaica." *Journal of Development Economics* 50(1): 165–87.

Hoddinott, J., and L. Haddad. 1995. "Does Female Income Share Influence Household Expenditures? Evidence from Côte d'Ivoire." *Oxford Bulletin of Economics and Statistics* 57(1): 77–95.

Inter-American Development Bank. 2007. *Outsiders? The Changing Patterns of Exclusion in Latin America and the Caribbean*. Washington DC: IADB.

Katayama, H., S. Lu, and J. Tybout. 2006. "Firm-level Productivity Studies: Illusions and a Solution." Mimeo. State College, Pa.: Department of Economics, Pennsylvania State University.

Kenyon, T. 2007. "A Framework for Thinking about Enterprise Formalization in Developing Countries." Policy Research Working Paper 4235. World Bank, Washington, DC.

Levine C. E., M. T. Ruel, and S. S. Morris, 1999. "Working Women in an Urban Setting: Traders, Vendors and Food Security in Accra." *World Development*, 27(11): 1977–91.

Lund, F., and C. Skinner, 2004. "The Investment Climate for the Informal Economy. The Case of Durban, South Africa." Background paper for the World Bank. WDR 2001. World Bank, Washington, DC.

Mayoux, L. 1995. "From Vicious to Virtuous Circles: Gender and Micro-Enterprise Development." Occasional Paper. New York: United Nations Development Program.

Mercado, A., and Ríos, F. 2005. "La Informalidad: ¿Estrategia de Sobrevivencia o Forma de Vida Alternativa?" Instituto de Investigaciones Socio-Económicas. Universidad Católica Boliviana. La Paz, Bolivia. April 2005.

Morrison, A., and M. B. Orlando. 2004. "The Costs and Impacts of Gender-based Violence in Developing Countries: Methodological Considerations and New Evidence." Working Paper. World Bank, Washington, DC.

———. 1999. "The Socioeconomic Costs of Domestic Violence: Chile and Nicaragua." In Morrison and Biehl, eds., *Too Close to Home: Domestic Violence in the Americas*. Washington, DC: IADB.

Morrison, A., M. Ellsberg, and S. Blott. 2004. "Addressing Gender-Based Violence in the Latin American and Caribbean Region: A Critical Review of Interventions." World Bank Policy Research Working Paper 3438. World Bank, Washington, DC.

Morrison, A., M. B. Orlando, and G. Pizzolitto. Forthcoming. "The Impact of Intimate Partner Violence against Women in Peru: Estimates using Matching Techniques." World Bank, Washington, DC.

Nadvi, K., and S. Barrientos. 2004. "Industrial Clusters and Poverty Reduction: Towards a Methodology for Poverty and Social Impact Assessment of Cluster Development Initiatives." Vienna, Austria: UNIDO.

Pagan, J., and S. Sanchez. 2000. "Gender Differences in Labor Market Decisions: Evidence from Rural Mexico." *Economic Development and Cultural Change* 48(3): 619–37.

Patrinos, H.A., E. Skoufias, and T. Lunde, 2007. "Indigenous Peoples in Latin America: Economic Opportunity and Social Networks." World Bank Policy Research Paper 4227. World Bank, Washington, DC.

Pena-Parga, X., and A. Glassman. 2004. "Demand For Child Care and Female Employment in Colombia." Documentos Cede 002267, Universidad De Los Andes-Cede.

Perry, Guillermo et al. 2007. *Informality: Exit and Exclusion*, Washington DC: World Bank.

Pitt, M., and S. Khandker. 1998. "The Impact of Group-Based Credit Programs on Poor Households in Bangladesh: Does the Gender of Participants Matter?" *Journal of Political Economy* 106.

Programa Nacional Violencia y Genero. 2004. "Prevención y Atención de Violencias: Plan Nacional 2004–2007." La Paz, Bolivia: Ministerio de Salud y Deporte.

Redfern, A., and P. Snedker. 2002. "Creating Market Opportunities for Small Enterprises: Experiences of the Fair Trade Movement." Geneva: ILO.

Ribero, R. 2003. "Gender Dimensions of Non-formal Employment in Colombia." Documento CEDE 2002–03.

Rogerson, C. 2004. "Pro-Poor Local Economic Development in Post-Apartheid South Africa, the Johannesburg Fashion District." *International Development Policy Review* 26(4).

Schultz, T. P. 2004. "School Subsidies for the Poor: Evaluating the Mexican *Progresa* Poverty Program." *Journal of Development Economics* 74(1).

———. 2002. "Why Governments Should Invest More to Educate Girls." *World Development* 30(2).

Sierra, G., and I. Calle. 2006. "Estudio sobre los Efectos de los Programas de Empleo de Emergencia en las Condiciones de las Mujeres Participantes: Lecciones aprendidads y opciones para la re-inserción al mercado laboral." Cooperación Técnica Belga, La Paz, Marzo.

Skinner, C. 2006. "The Informal Sector in South Africa: Trends and Policy Challenges." Presentation given at the eThekwini Informal Economy Conference, November 9, 2006.

Skoufias, E., and S. Parker. 2001. "Conditional Cash Transfers and their Impact on Child Work and School Enrollment: Evidence from the *Progresa* Program in Mexico." *Economia* 2(1).

Stephen, L. 2005. *Zapotec Women: Gender, Class, and Ethnicity in Globalized Oaxaca*, 2nd Rev Upd edition. Durham: Duke University Press.

Tannuri-Pianto, M., and D. Pianto. 2003. *Formal, Informal and Self-employed Earnings in Urban Bolivia: Accounting for Sample Selection with Multiple-Choice Models*. July 2003.

Tannuri-Pianto, M., D. Pianto, and O. Arias. 2004. "Informal Employment in Bolivia: A Lost Proposition?" Mimeo.

Thomas, D. 1990. "Intra-Household Resource Allocation: An Inferential Approach." *The Journal of Human Resources* 25: 635–64.

Tokman, V. 2001. "Integrating the Informal Sector in the Modernization Process." *SAIS Review* 21(1), Winter-Spring.

Tzannatos, Z. 2004. "Ethnicity and the Labor Market in LAC: A Study of Employment and Earnings over Time in Bolivia, Guatemala, Mexico and Peru." Background paper for *Indigenous People, Poverty and Human Development in Latin America: 1994–2004*. Washington DC: World Bank.

Valdivia, M., and D. Karlan. 2006. "Teaching Entrepreneurship: Impact of Business Training on Microfinance Clients and Institutions." Working Paper 941. Economic Growth Center, Yale University.

Vegas, E., P. Cerdan-Infantes, E. Dunkelberg, E. Molina. 2006. "Evidencia Internacional sobre Políticas de la Primera Infancia que Estimulen el Desarrollo Infantil y Faciliten la Inserción Laboral Femenina." Documento de Trabajo. World Bank, Washington, DC.

Vidaurre, G. 2005. "Impacto de la importación de ropa usada en Bolivia." La Paz: Instituto Boliviano de Comercio Exterior (IBCE).

WBCSD. 2004. "Daimler Chrysler and POEMAtec Alliance: Partnering for Mutual Success." Case Study, World Business Council for Sustainable Development, http://www.wbcsd.org/web/publications/case/daimlerchrysler_poematec_full_case_web.pdf.

Wong, R., and R. Levine. 1992. "Household Structures as a Response to Economic Adjustments: Evidence from the 1980`s Urban Mexico." *Estudios Demograficos y Urbanos* 7: 2–3.

World Bank. 2005. "Bolivia Poverty Assessment: Establishing the Basis for Pro-poor Growth." World Bank, Washington, DC.

——. 2004. "Labor Market Regulations for Women: Are they Beneficial?" PREMNotes No. 94, World Bank, Washington, DC.

——. 2006. "Basic Education in Bolivia: Challenges for 2006–2010." World Bank, Washington, DC.

——. 2007a. *Policies for Increasing Firms' Formality and Productivity*. Washington DC: World Bank.

——. 2007b. *Global Monitoring Report 2007*. Washington DC: World Bank.

# Appendixes

## Appendix 1. Estimation Methods

We consider three approaches to measure the impact of formality on profitability. Our methods include (i) an ordinary least squares regression (OLS); (ii) a Treatment Effects regression that tries to take account of the potential endogeneity of formality; and (iii) an estimate using propensity score matching.

### Methodology for the OLS regression

The ordinary least squares regression is based on the following equation:

$$\ln\left(PROFITS\right)_i = \lambda + \alpha\,Firms'Characteristics_i + \beta\,Owners'Characteristics_i$$
$$+\gamma\,Industry_i + \delta\,Location_i + \theta\,Formal_i + \varepsilon_i$$

The outcome of interest here is $\theta$, which measures the average increase in log profits associated with being formal, conditional on the other variables included in the regression. Assigning a causal interpretation to formality based on this estimation requires assuming selection on the observable variables included in this equation, as well as assuming that the linear functional form adequately captures profits.

A key concern with OLS estimation of equation (2) is that the error term $\varepsilon$ is correlated with formality. There are several possible reasons for this concern. First, if we exclude firm size from (2), we would expect a positive bias, due to larger firms earning higher profits and also being more likely to be formal. In the OLS results we should therefore expect the estimate of $\theta$ to become less positive as we include firm size. Second, a concern is that $\varepsilon$ may include unmeasured ability of the firm, with higher ability leading to more profits and also affecting the decision to become formal. If ability is a complement to formality, we should again expect this to lead to an upward bias in $\theta$. This is what we found among smaller firms. However, among larger firms there appeared to be a negative relationship between (measured) ability and formality. For these firms, ability may be a substitute for formality. Able owners may have no trouble attracting customers and financing and perhaps are also more successful at avoiding fines. Thus, among larger firms we might expect a downward bias in $\theta$. The overall bias when we pool firms is therefore unclear.

### Methodology for the Treatment Effects regression

A second approach to estimation is to try and take account of the potential endogeneity of formality by instrumenting for formality status when estimating (2). Since formality is a binary variable, we use STATA's treatreg command to fit a maximum-likelihood Treatment Effects model. The instrument we rely on is the distance from the firm to the location of the office where the firm would have to register. As shown in the previous section, distance to the SIN office strongly predicts whether a firm has a tax number.[1] However, distance to the Alcaldia office is not a strong predictor of whether a firm has a municipal license, conditional on the other variables included in this regression. A possible reason for this is that the municipality is more active in both disseminating information about how to register and also in enforcement. In contrast, many firms lack information about where the SIN office is or how to get a tax number. Thus we can only use this treatment effects model for modeling the impact of a tax number, not the impact of a municipal license.

The *t*-statistic on log distance to the SIN office is around 3.8, after conditioning on the other variables in the regression. If we restrict to firms within 10 kilometers of the SIN office, this drops to 3.5, which is still strong and significant. Thus, this distance instrument provides a strong first stage.

The exclusion restriction we rely on here is that, conditional on the distance of a firm to the city center, and the average tax enforcement in a firm's city and industry pair, distance to the SIN office has no direct impact on profitability. One possible reason this assumption could be violated would be if firms choose where to operate with the location of the SIN office in mind. However, as previously discussed, a majority of firms do not know where the SIN office is, and many firms operate out of their homes. Within a large city it seems that the location of the tax office is not a main concern when deciding where to locate.

**Methodology for the propensity score matching**
Finally, to complement the OLS and Treatment Effects regressions, we also provide estimates of the impact of being formal on profits using propensity score matching. Propensity score matching assumes that all selection occurs on observables, but does not require assuming a linear function form. Additionally, use of propensity score matching allows us to estimate the impact of a municipal license, for which we do not have an instrumental variable. We use the same variables as in the OLS regressions, along with higher-order interaction terms in carrying out the match.

## Appendix 2. Do the Factors That Affect Formality Vary by Gender?

| | Municipal License | | | | NIT | | | |
| --- | --- | --- | --- | --- | --- | --- | --- | --- |
| | w/o size control | | with size control | | w/o size control | | with size control | |
| | (1) | (2) | (3) | (4) | (1) | (2) | (3) | (4) |
| | Males | Females | Males | Females | Males | Females | Males | Females |
| Age | 0.00113 | 0.00631* | 0.00194 | 0.00478 | 0.00662** | 0.000564 | 0.00682** | 0.000652 |
| | (0.0030) | (0.0035) | (0.0033) | (0.0039) | (0.0029) | (0.0018) | (0.0028) | (0.00070) |
| Married | 0.0991 | 0.0597 | 0.0640 | 0.119 | 0.0964 | -0.0139 | 0.00586 | -0.00697 |
| | (0.077) | (0.077) | (0.083) | (0.083) | (0.069) | (0.042) | (0.072) | (0.016) |
| Indigenous language as child | 0.0868 | -0.0845 | 0.0536 | -0.110 | 0.0464 | -0.0345 | 0.0531 | -0.0183 |
| | (0.087) | (0.088) | (0.098) | (0.094) | (0.088) | (0.047) | (0.091) | (0.018) |
| Post secondary education | 0.0844 | -0.106 | 0.0681 | -0.0587 | 0.110 | -0.0344 | 0.0632 | -0.0104 |
| | (0.076) | (0.091) | (0.084) | (0.10) | (0.076) | (0.040) | (0.075) | (0.013) |
| Basico education | 0.0748 | 0.0228 | 0.115 | 0.0765 | 0.0769 | -0.0756 | 0.0741 | -0.0203 |
| | (0.10) | (0.095) | (0.11) | (0.10) | (0.11) | (0.046) | (0.11) | (0.019) |
| Self-efficacy | 0.0225 | 0.0285 | 0.0173 | 0.0293 | 0.0441** | 0.0213* | 0.0282 | 0.00531 |
| | (0.019) | (0.021) | (0.020) | (0.024) | (0.018) | (0.012) | (0.018) | (0.0055) |
| In business to Care for Family | -0.175** | -0.0367 | -0.156* | -0.130 | -0.171** | -0.00637 | -0.124* | 0.0122 |
| | (0.074) | (0.090) | (0.081) | (0.10) | (0.070) | (0.046) | (0.070) | (0.014) |
| In business for flexible hours | 0.0565 | 0.00537 | 0.0592 | 0.110 | -0.0112 | -0.0469 | -0.0258 | -0.00400 |
| | (0.073) | (0.080) | (0.081) | (0.085) | (0.072) | (0.046) | (0.071) | (0.015) |
| In business for growth | -0.0796 | 0.129* | -0.124 | 0.0877 | 0.161*** | 0.0318 | 0.0811 | -0.00754 |
| | (0.072) | (0.078) | (0.077) | (0.086) | (0.062) | (0.041) | (0.062) | (0.017) |
| Child poverty | 0.00395 | -0.0410 | -0.00592 | -0.0211 | -0.0208 | -0.00577 | -0.0289 | 0.00204 |
| | (0.029) | (0.032) | (0.031) | (0.036) | (0.027) | (0.016) | (0.026) | (0.0058) |
| Father owned a business | 0.140** | 0.00152 | 0.0975 | 0.0136 | 0.0574 | 0.0226 | -0.0174 | 0.00305 |
| | (0.071) | (0.081) | (0.078) | (0.089) | (0.072) | (0.044) | (0.066) | (0.016) |
| Average tax inspection rate | 0.104 | 0.543 | -0.212 | 0.653 | 2.312*** | 0.480 | 2.005*** | 0.196 |
| | (0.58) | (0.63) | (0.62) | (0.71) | (0.61) | (0.33) | (0.58) | (0.16) |
| El Alto | -0.254** | 0.00275 | -0.159 | 0.0988 | -0.0603 | -0.119*** | 0.104 | -0.0253 |
| | (0.11) | (0.12) | (0.12) | (0.14) | (0.094) | (0.046) | (0.12) | (0.023) |
| La Paz | -0.0987 | -0.0199 | -0.0291 | 0.137 | -0.201** | -0.0916* | -0.137 | -0.0104 |
| | (0.13) | (0.14) | (0.13) | (0.17) | (0.091) | (0.053) | (0.084) | (0.022) |
| Cochabamba | -0.0634 | 0.161 | -0.0244 | 0.285** | -0.174* | -0.0167 | -0.124 | 0.00492 |
| | (0.13) | (0.12) | (0.13) | (0.13) | (0.093) | (0.059) | (0.085) | (0.023) |
| Food | -0.0391 | -0.210** | -0.0792 | -0.317*** | 0.217 | -0.0156 | 0.0704 | -0.0130 |
| | (0.19) | (0.082) | (0.25) | (0.088) | (0.19) | (0.044) | (0.21) | (0.015) |
| Clothing | -0.200 | -0.339*** | -0.337 | -0.413*** | 0.189 | -0.0530 | -0.0333 | -0.00893 |
| | (0.20) | (0.098) | (0.22) | (0.087) | (0.19) | (0.061) | (0.16) | (0.021) |
| Wood | -0.240 | 0.358* | -0.401* | -0.0501 | 0.221 | 0.502** | -0.0432 | 0.143 |
| | (0.20) | (0.21) | (0.22) | (0.27) | (0.19) | (0.24) | (0.16) | (0.21) |
| Camelid | -0.582*** | -0.450** | -0.575*** | -0.530*** | 0.684*** | 0.0879 | 0.802*** | 0.0286 |
| | (0.13) | (0.19) | (0.13) | (0.16) | (0.17) | (0.20) | (0.15) | (0.092) |
| Transport | -0.183 | | -0.365 | | 0.543** | 0.133 | 0.378 | |
| | (0.24) | | (0.26) | | (0.21) | (0.25) | (0.28) | |
| Log distance to city | 0.0259 | -0.180*** | 0.0280 | -0.211*** | 0.167*** | -0.0148 | 0.148** | -0.00841 |
| | (0.052) | (0.056) | (0.058) | (0.067) | (0.062) | (0.031) | (0.063) | (0.011) |
| Log distance to alcaldia | -0.0478 | 0.149** | -0.0319 | 0.234*** | | | | |
| | (0.053) | (0.058) | (0.059) | (0.072) | | | | |
| Log distance to SIN | | | | | -0.237*** | -0.0499* | -0.211*** | -0.0136 |
| | | | | | (0.063) | (0.029) | (0.063) | (0.011) |
| One to four workers | | | 0.147* | 0.248** | | | 0.311*** | 0.0340 |
| | | | (0.085) | (0.096) | | | (0.089) | (0.030) |
| Five to ten workers | | | 0.243** | 0.313** | | | 0.607*** | 0.321** |
| | | | (0.10) | (0.14) | | | (0.13) | (0.16) |
| Log Capital Stock | | | 0.0498* | 0.0470** | | | 0.0801*** | 0.0141* |
| | | | (0.028) | (0.022) | | | (0.026) | (0.0085) |
| Eleven or more workers | | | 0.156 | | | | 0.549** | |
| | | | (0.20) | | | | (0.25) | |
| Observations | 266 | 286 | 242 | 252 | 266 | 291 | 242 | 252 |

Standard errors in parentheses
*** p<0.01, ** p<0.05, * p<0.1

## Appendix 3. Does the Impact of a NIT (and Other Factors) on Profits Vary by Gender?

| | OLS Results | | | | Maximum-Likelihood Results | | | |
| --- | --- | --- | --- | --- | --- | --- | --- | --- |
| | w/o size control | | with size control | | w/o size control | | with size control | |
| | (1) | (2) | (3) | (4) | (5) | (6) | (7) | (8) |
| | Males | Females | Males | Females | Males | Females | Males | Females |
| NIT | 0.359 | 0.504 | -0.047 | 0.194 | 0.507 | 0.198 | 0.045 | 0.536 |
| | (2.54)* | (2.54)* | (0.37) | (0.85) | (1.29) | (0.32) | (0.15) | (1.24) |
| Age | -0.009 | -0.002 | -0.001 | -0.005 | -0.010 | -0.003 | -0.002 | -0.005 |
| | (1.73) | (0.37) | (0.24) | (0.73) | (1.74) | (0.44) | (0.31) | (0.76) |
| Young firm | -0.077 | -0.225 | 0.032 | -0.135 | -0.066 | -0.268 | 0.034 | -0.095 |
| | (0.55) | (1.32) | (0.25) | (0.79) | (0.49) | (1.59) | (0.29) | (0.61) |
| Married | 0.208 | 0.010 | 0.094 | 0.104 | 0.193 | 0.011 | 0.091 | 0.096 |
| | (1.42) | (0.07) | (0.69) | (0.69) | (1.40) | (0.07) | (0.76) | (0.67) |
| Indigenous language | 0.230 | 0.001 | 0.241 | -0.007 | 0.221 | -0.015 | 0.239 | 0.015 |
| | (1.32) | (0.01) | (1.41) | (0.04) | (1.43) | (0.09) | (1.69) | (0.09) |
| Post Secondary Education | 0.268 | 0.108 | 0.202 | 0.151 | 0.250 | 0.088 | 0.197 | 0.179 |
| | (1.99)* | (0.52) | (1.53) | (0.78) | (1.79) | (0.49) | (1.61) | (1.00) |
| Basico Education | -0.115 | 0.223 | 0.011 | 0.275 | -0.116 | 0.198 | 0.005 | 0.295 |
| | (0.54) | (1.27) | (0.06) | (1.54) | (0.61) | (1.17) | (0.03) | (1.83) |
| Child poverty | 0.001 | -0.139 | -0.052 | -0.078 | 0.002 | 0.098 | -0.050 | -0.084 |
| | (0.01) | (2.54)* | (3.28)** | (1.41) | (0.03) | (2.26)* | (1.13) | (1.96)* |
| Self-efficacy | 0.123 | 0.086 | 0.091 | 0.084 | 0.116 | -0.136 | 0.088 | 0.076 |
| | (4.00)** | (2.05)* | (1.03) | (2.00)* | (3.12)** | (2.29)* | (2.84)** | (1.40) |
| In business to Care for Family | -0.215 | -0.265 | -0.099 | -0.280 | -0.199 | -0.263 | -0.093 | -0.290 |
| | (1.60) | (1.65) | (0.79) | (1.68) | (1.45) | (1.70) | (0.78) | (1.87) |
| In business for flexible hours | -0.146 | 0.058 | -0.118 | 0.160 | -0.150 | 0.058 | -0.122 | 0.151 |
| | (1.09) | (0.38) | (0.93) | (1.00) | (1.18) | (0.41) | (1.05) | (1.04) |
| In business for growth | -0.092 | 0.179 | -0.054 | 0.107 | -0.114 | 0.176 | -0.062 | 0.110 |
| | (0.71) | (1.18) | (0.45) | (0.70) | (0.81) | (1.25) | (0.52) | (0.78) |
| Father owned a business | -0.203 | -0.231 | -0.317 | -0.223 | -0.205 | -0.239 | -0.316 | -0.210 |
| | (1.57) | (1.53) | (2.71)** | (1.41) | (1.61) | (1.61) | (2.76)** | (1.42) |
| Log distance to city | 0.012 | -0.101 | 0.057 | -0.067 | 0.016 | -0.116 | 0.059 | -0.055 |
| | (0.27) | (2.19)* | (1.33) | (1.38) | (0.35) | (2.09)* | (1.39) | (1.10) |
| Average tax inspection rate | -1.798 | -1.163 | -1.822 | -1.056 | | | | |
| | (1.88) | (0.98) | (2.35)* | (0.87) | | | | |
| One to four workers | | | 0.183 | 0.195 | | | 0.169 | 0.163 |
| | | | (1.15) | (1.14) | | | (1.24) | (1.07) |
| Five to ten workers | | | 0.796 | 0.673 | | | 0.773 | 0.546 |
| | | | (3.69)** | (2.66)** | | | (4.01)** | (1.94) |
| Eleven or more workers | | | 0.719 | 1.037 | | | 0.696 | 0.822 |
| | | | (2.01)* | (1.62) | | | (2.23)* | (1.14) |
| Log capital stock | | | 0.202 | 0.102 | | | 0.194 | 0.094 |
| | | | (4.17)** | (2.82)** | | | (3.91)** | (2.83)** |
| Constant | 8.036 | 7.015 | 5.378 | 5.959 | 8.085 | 7.035 | 5.495 | 6.041 |
| | (17.67)** | (14.39)** | (8.82)** | (10.56)** | (17.52)** | (14.54)** | (7.74)** | (10.88)** |
| | | | | | | | | |
| Observations | 244 | 244 | 224 | 223 | 244 | 244 | 224 | 223 |
| R-squared | 0.31 | 0.26 | 0.47 | 0.32 | | | | |

Robust t statistics in parentheses
* significant at 5%; ** significant at 1%

## Appendix 4. Interest Rates for Microcredit Institutions in Latin America (June 2005)

| | | |
|---|---|---|
| FINCOMUN | Mexico | 114,26% |
| COMPARTAMOS | Mexico | 100,18% |
| FDD | Rep.Dominicana | 83,65% |
| ADOPEM | Rep.Dominicana | 67,07% |
| IDESI LA LIBERTAD | Peru | 63,05% |
| FRAC | Mexico | 61,24% |
| PROMUJER | Nicaragua | 58,34% |
| ADRA PERU | Peru | 57,86% |
| PROMUJER PERU | Peru | 56,67% |
| D-MIRO | Ecuador | 46,08% |
| CREAR AREQUIPA | Peru | 45,34% |
| PROCREDIT | Nicaragua | 43,68% |
| MIDE | Peru | 43,22% |
| EL COMERCIO | Paraguay | 43,00% |
| CONFIANZA | Peru | 42,36% |
| WWB POPAYAN | Colombia | 41,84% |
| CMAC SULLANA | Peru | 41,73% |
| WWB BOGOTA | Colombia | 41,68% |
| EDYFICAR | Peru | 41,15% |
| PROMUJER BOLIVIA | Bolivia | 39,83% |
| PROEMPRESA | Peru | 39,74% |
| NIEBOROWSKI | Nicaragua | 39,25% |
| NUEVA VISION | Peru | 39,11% |
| CREAR TACNA | Peru | 39,00% |
| CMAC ICA | Peru | 38,84% |
| WWB CALI | Colombia | 37,55% |
| WWB BUCARAMANGA | Colombia | 35,60% |
| AMC | El Salvador | 35,54% |
| FUNDESER | Nicaragua | 34,89% |
| CMAC AREQUIPA | Peru | 32,63% |
| CMAC TRUJILLO | Peru | 31,50% |
| WWB MEDELLIN | Colombia | 31,41% |
| CMAC TACNA | Peru | 30,06% |
| D-FRIF | Bolivia | 29,71% |
| CMAC CUSCO | Peru | 28,15% |
| BANCO PROCREDIT | El Salvador | 21,53% |
| ASOFIN (1) | Bolivia | 21,23% |
| FADES | Bolivia | 20,71% |

*Source*: World Bank 2007.

## Appendix 5. Mutually Reinforcing Constraints on Female Micro Enterprises

|  | Macro-level | Household Level | Individual |
|---|---|---|---|
| Resources and property | Unequal inheritance laws, inequality in marriage contract and community access to land | Male appropriation of household/family property | Lack of individual property |
| Income | Legal systems that treat women as dependants rather than individuals, also reflected in tax and benefit systems<br>Lack of public welfare provision or recognition of costs of reproductive services<br>Low female wages | Male appropriation of incomes<br>Female responsibility for family provisioning and male withdrawal of income | Lack of control over incomes<br>Prioritization of investment in household<br>Low incomes for investment |
| Credit | Financial system discriminating against women | Male appropriation of credit | Lack of collateral |
| Skills | Lack of opportunities for apprenticeship<br>Gender-stereotyped training and education that devalues women<br>Discrimination in access to education system and training | Lack of investment in female education and skill acquisition of female skills<br>Low valuation of female skills | Lack of confidence and ability to enter new areas of activity |
| Marketing | Lack of access to marketing support<br>Lack of marketing support for female-dominated industries<br>Harassment of female informal sector workers | Concern with family honor and restrictions on female mobility | Lack of information and networks |
| Labor | Unwillingness of men to work under a woman firm owners | Limited claim to unpaid male family labor<br>Women's responsibility for unpaid family labor | Lack of networks and authority<br>Lack of time |
| General underlying constraints | Institutionalized discrimination and violence<br>Lack of women's participation in decision-making | Opposition to female independence and autonomy<br>Domestic violence | Lack of autonomy<br>Lack of confidence |

*Source*: Mayoux, 2001, Chen et al 2004.

## Notes

[1] Further evidence for the validity of the assumption that distance to the SIN office is picking up information about getting an NIT rather than some general location characteristic affecting the incentives for formality is seen in the fact that distance to the SIN office does not significantly predict which firms get a municipal license or register with Fundaempresa.

# Eco-Audit

## Environmental Benefits Statement

The World Bank is committed to preserving Endangered Forests and natural resources. We print World Bank Working Papers and Country Studies on postconsumer recycled paper, processed chlorine free. The World Bank has formally agreed to follow the recommended standards for paper usage set by Green Press Initiative—a nonprofit program supporting publishers in using fiber that is not sourced from Endangered Forests. For more information, visit www.greenpressinitiative.org.

In 2008, the printing of these books on recycled paper saved the following:

| Trees* | Solid Waste | Water | Net Greenhouse Gases | Total Energy |
|---|---|---|---|---|
| 355 | 16,663 | 129,550 | 31,256 | 247 mil. |
| *40 feet in height and 6–8 inches in diameter | Pounds | Gallons | Pounds CO$_2$ Equivalent | BTUs |